OAKWOOD LIBRARY OF RAILWAY HISTORY

THE KINGTON LINES
FROM LEOMINSTER TO KINGTON AND NEW RADNOR
INCLUDING THE BRANCHES TO PRESTEIGNE AND EARDISLEY

John Mair

View of Kingsland station looking towards Pembridge. *John Alsop collection*

THE OAKWOOD PRESS

© John Mair, 2023

ISBN 978-0-85361-770-9

First Published in the United Kingdom, 2023.

Printed by
Claro Print, Office 26, 27, 1 Spiersbridge Way
Thornliebank, Glasgow G46 8NG

In Memoriam

Colin H. Betts

Colleague, Mentor, Friend

Arrival at New Radnor. Alighting passengers and luggage are being prepared for the last lap of the journey to the village. *Lens of Sutton Association*

Published by
The Oakwood Press, 54-58 Mill Square, Catrine, KA5 6RD
01290 551122   www.stenlake.co.uk

Contents

Preface 4

One   **Historical Outline** 5
Early Transport in West Herefordshire, 5; Tram roads to Hay and Kington, 6; Proposals for Railways, 10; The Shrewsbury and Hereford Railway, 10; The Leominster and Kington Railway, 12; Construction of the Leominster and Kington Railway, 14; The line opens, 16; Along the line, 18; Early years, 19; The Hereford, Hay and Brecon Railway, 20; A practical plan, 20; The Kington and Eardisley Railway, 21; Eardisley, 26; The New Radnor Extension, 26; Alterations at Kington, 28: The Presteigne Branch, 31; The Worcester, Bromyard and Leominster Railway, 33; The Twentieth Century, 35; The First World War …, 35; … and its Aftermath, 36; The 'Country Lorry' initiative, 38; The Second World War, 39; Peace … and Nationalisation, 39; 'The Kington Centenary Rail Tour', 41

Two   **Operation of the Lines** 43
Gradients, *From Leominster to New Radnor*, 43; *From Titley to Eardisley*, 44; *From Titley to Presteigne*, 44: Passenger train services, 45; Eardisley, 46; Passenger rolling stock, 49; The Second World War …, 52; … and its aftermath, 55; The Worcester connection, 55: Goods traffic, 58; The Old Radnor Trading Company Limited, 59; Marston siding, 60; Goods traffic ends, 60: Motive Power, 60; Engine Sheds, *Leominster*, 62; *Kington*, 64: Signalling, *Methods*, 65; *Kington Junction*, 67; *Kingsland*, 68; *Pembridge*, 69; *Titley*, 72; *Kington and the New Radnor Extension*, 74; *The line to Eardisley*, 75; *The Presteigne Branch*, 76; *Signal box hours of opening*, 76; Speed Restrictions, 76

Three   **A Journey Over the Lines in the 1930s** 77
Leominster to Kington, 77; On to New Radnor, 87; From Titley Junction to Presteigne, 93; Presteigne station, 94; From Titley Junction to Eardisley, 95

Epilogue 99
Bibliography 101
Index 103

Preface

To this day the countryside of West Herefordshire retains an Arcadian character: its gently undulating landform is threaded by limpid streams and its picturesque villages and orchards are set amid pastoral and arable scenes of great natural beauty. Further west lies the perhaps more severe landscape of the Radnorshire hills. Beyond, and still further west, are the Cambrian Mountains, so inviting and yet so resistant to railway communication.

It is almost startling to find that this remote area, resembling a small, self-contained, kingdom, was one of the first in Britain to be served by a long distance tramway: as early as 1820 the combined Hay and Kington Railways ran for 36 miles to connect a canal wharf at Brecon with the limestone quarries at Burlingjobb, west of Kington. In their quiet way these conjoined tramways paved the way for a fascinating system of standard gauge railways whose origins, development, operations and decline I have tried to describe in this book.

It has become customary to spell the name of the county town of the former Radnorshire as 'Presteigne', and that is the usage which is followed in this book. The railway companies and British Railways (Western Region) did, however, habitually use the form 'Presteign', and that is the spelling which will be found in some of the extracts taken from railway literature.

I gratefully record my thanks to my friend the late Colin Betts, and to my pen friend the late Jack Burrell, both of whom encouraged and indeed inspired my original interest in the area. More recently, Michael Clemens has provided invaluable help and information, photographs, and extracts from the diaries of the late Eric Parker. I am also grateful to Reg Instone, John Lacy, and Garth Tilt of the Signalling Record Society and to Tony Cooke for their always generously given assistance; and to John Alsop, Deborah Esher of the Middleton Press, Nicky Harden, the Lens of Sutton Association, Colin Maggs, and Laurence Waters of the Great Western Trust for providing many of the photographs which appear in the book. And once again I offer warm thanks to Lewis Hutton, designer at the Oakwood Press, for his continuing guidance and encouragement. Lewis also drew the maps/diagrams on pages 7, 19, 23 and 34, and compiled the index.

John Mair
Stanmore, Middlesex
October, 2023

Chapter One

Historical Outline

Early Transport in West Herefordshire

The latter part of the eighteenth century was the heyday of canal development in mainland Britain. Many schemes were proposed, and some were implemented, either wholly or in part. A prolific designer and builder of canals was Robert Whitworth, who had been an assistant to John Smeaton and James Brindley, two of the most eminent engineers of the age.

In 1777 Robert Whitworth proposed the construction of an entirely new canal which would begin at a junction with the Staffordshire and Worcestershire Canal at Stourport-on-Severn, run westwards towards the Teme Valley (south of the Wyre Forest), and then southwards to Leominster and to Hereford. From there it would proceed eastwards to Ledbury, and finally return to the River Severn below Tewkesbury. This route would thus describe a grand arc, connecting many small towns and villages as well as the larger centres, and providing them with an outlet for their agricultural and horticultural produce, timber, and minerals such as limestone. Goods inwards would consist chiefly of coal, which, in the absence of gas and electricity, was required all the year round for domestic and industrial purposes; and of manufactured products from the West Midlands. An Act to authorise the canal received Royal Assent on 13th May, 1791. The legislation provided for the construction of a canal branch from north of Leominster to Kington, near the western boundary of Herefordshire. Kington would thus gain access to and from the Midlands, and obtain an outlet for the products of its foundry and woollen mills, as well as for agricultural produce; and for the limestone which was quarried and for the lime which was produced in nearby Radnorshire. Such an addition was technically quite feasible, and indeed work was started upon building an aqueduct for the extension to cross the River Lugg near Kingsland, west of Leominster.

In the event, however, the only – and land-locked – section of the northern part of Whitworth's proposed canal to be completed was that between Marlbrook (in Worcestershire) and Leominster, a distance of approximately 18½ miles. This length came into use as far as Woofferton in October, 1794, and then to Leominster in December, 1796. In the vicinity of the village of Mamble, to the east of the start of the canal at Marlbrook, were several modestly-sized but productive collieries, and coal thus gained was conveyed by a tram road to a wharf on what became known as the 'Leominster Canal': when canal-borne coal became available in the town of that name, the price per ton fell by 50 per cent from 30s. to 15s. per ton.

The planned continuations to Hereford and to Kington did not, however, materialise, and the initial work on the aqueduct (above) was abandoned. Kington never received a canal; West Herefordshire generally remained isolated; and a later scheme to build a tram road between Kington and a proposed, but never built, canal terminus at Kingsland, about 3 miles west of Leominster, was not pursued. Further south, the Herefordshire and Gloucestershire Navigation Company eventually completed a canal from Hereford, via Ledbury and Newent, to the River Severn opposite Gloucester.

Tram Roads to Hay and Kington

In the longer term, some relief was to become available, although from a quite unexpected and indirect source. The Monmouthshire Canal ran northwards from Newport, and at Pontymoile (near Pontypool) it formed a junction with the Brecon and Abergavenny Canal. This latter canal, which was opened on 24th December, 1800, terminated in a district called Watton, situated to the south of the centre of Brecon. From Watton a tram road – 'The Hay Railway' – was authorised by Acts of Parliament passed in 1811 and in 1812 to run to Hay, in the Wye Valley, and then to the village of Eardisley, a distance of 24¼ miles from Brecon. This tram road was built in stages: it was opened as far as Hay on 14th May, 1816, and was then progressively extended to Eardisley, reached on 1st December, 1818. The line was built to a gauge of three feet and six inches and carried horse-drawn wagons.

Doubtless encouraged by the success of this initiative, some leading citizens of Kington met in 1817 and resolved to promote a similar tram road, of the same gauge, which would connect with the Hay Railway at Eardisley, and from there would cross the ridge between the valleys of the River Wye and of the River Arrow to reach Kington and the limestone quarries and works in the district known as Burlingjobb (also spelt Burlinjobb or Burlinjob). The southern end of the line would be situated on the *east* side of the main road (the modern A4111) running through Eardisley, and the proprietors of the Hay Railway co-operated in agreeing to extend their own line from the *west* side of the village to meet the Kington line at an end-on junction to permit of continuous

HISTORICAL OUTLINE

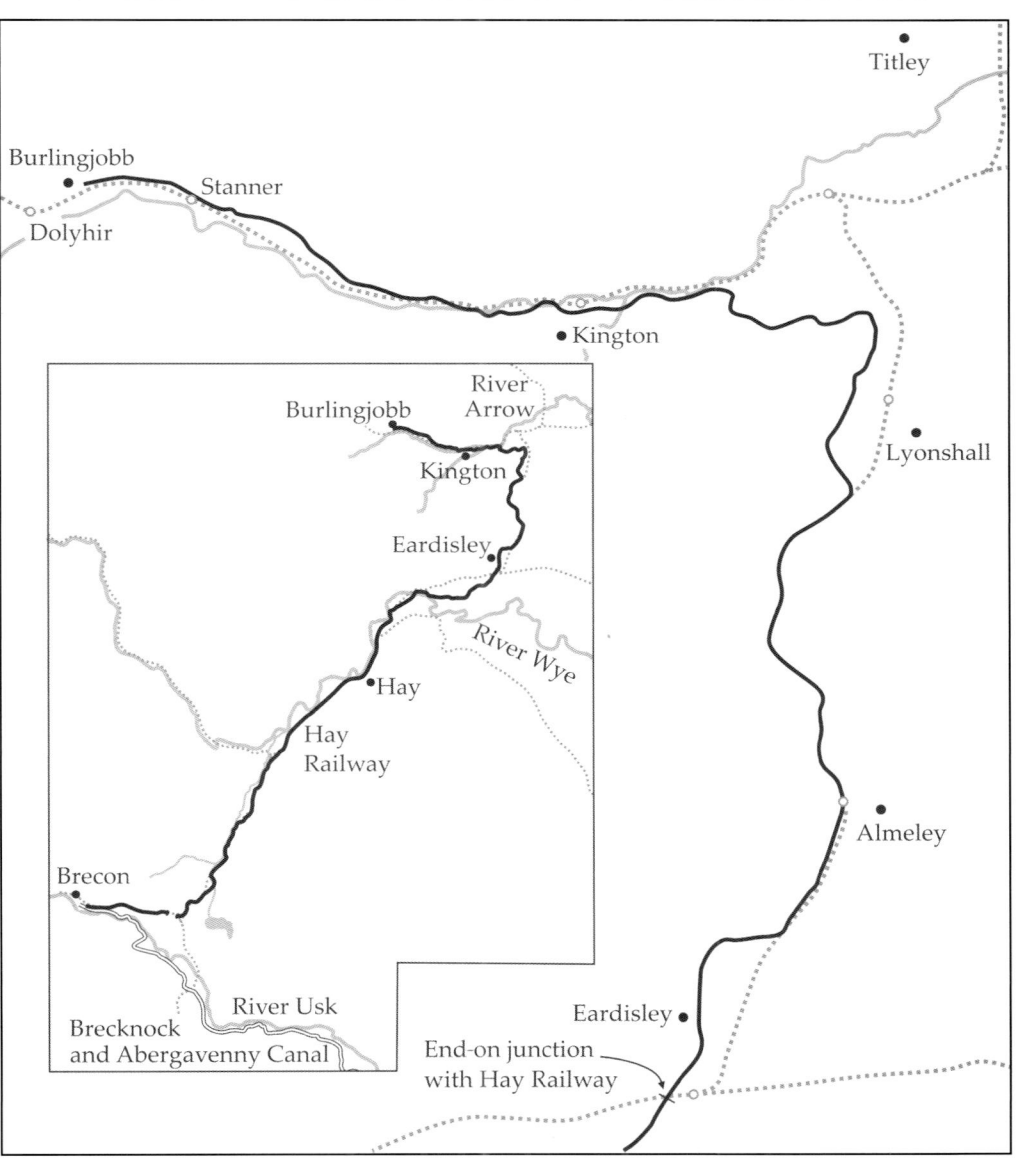

The Kington Railway showing the route from Burlingjobb to Eardisley. The later railways are shown in grey dotted lines. The inset map shows both the Kington and Hay Railways and their route to the Brecknock and Abergavenny Canal at Brecon, connecting the Arrow, Wye and Usk river valleys.

ANNO QUINQUAGESIMO OCTAVO

GEORGII III. REGIS.

****

Cap. lxiii.

An Act for making a Railway from the *Hay* Railway near *Eardisley*, in the County of *Hereford*, to the Lime Works near *Burlinjob*, in the County of *Radnor*.   [23d *May* 1818.]

WHEREAS the making and maintaining a Railway or Tram Road for the Passage of Waggons and other Carriages from the *Hay* Railway, at or near to the Village of *Eardisley*, in the Parish of *Eardisley*, in the County of *Hereford*, to or near to the Town of *Kington* in the said County, and from thence to or near to certain Lime Works at or near to the Village of *Burlinjob*, in the County of *Radnor*, will be of great public Utility, by facilitating and cheapening the Conveyance of Coal, Iron, and other Commodities from the County of *Brecon* to the said Town of *Kington* and the said Lime Works, and the Conveyance of Lime, Corn, and other Commodities from the said Town and Lime Works respectively, towards and into the said County of *Brecon* ; and by greatly relieving the Turnpike and other Roads in the Neighbourhood, which are at present in a very ruinous State, and cannot be kept in Repair by reason of the increased and increasing Carriage of heavy Goods thereon ; and will materially assist the Agricultural Interest, as well as the general Traffic of the Country, and tend to the Improvement of the Estates in the Vicinity of the said Railway or Tram Road : And whereas the several Persons herein-after named are willing and desirous at their own Expence to make and maintain the said Railway or Tram Road, and such other Works as are herein-after mentioned ; but the same cannot be effected without the Authority of Parliament : May it therefore please Your Majesty that it may be enacted ; and be it enacted

[*Local.*]   16 C   by

running between Brecon, Hay, Eardisley, Kington, and the limestone area.

Matters now proceeded with surprising speed. The necessary Act of Parliament (the Kington Railway Act) to incorporate the Kington Railway Company, to set out its financial structure, and to authorise the construction of the tramway, received Royal Assent on 23rd May, 1818. The authorised capital was £18,000 in the form of £100 shares. On 25th July, 1818, the proprietors decided to award to the firm of Hazledine and Sayce the contract to build the tramway (or tram road, as it became known) and by the end of that year appreciable progress had been made on the ground.

Work continued throughout 1819 and in the early part of 1820. The connecting line between the termini of the two tramways at Eardisley was built by John Hodgkinson, who was at various times the engineer for the Hay Railway (and who had unsuccessfully tendered for the construction of the Kington Railway). This connecting line remained the property of the Hay Railway Company, until the latter was purchased, in 1860, by the Hereford, Hay and Brecon Railway Company.

The new tram road was opened as far as the Floodgates (at the western end of Kington) on Monday, 1st May, 1820, and then throughout, to Burlingjobb, on Monday, 7th August in the same year. When opened, the resultant continuous tramway, measuring some 36 miles between the Watton wharf at Brecon and Burlingjobb, was easily the longest such line in the United Kingdom, and was withal situated in one of the most remote parts of lowland Britain.

There was now a link between this remote area and the mines, quarries and ironworks of Monmouthshire. The Monmouthshire Canal and the Brecon and Abergavenny Canal united to form a single waterway between the industrialised areas of south-east Monmouthshire and a wharf below Brecon, from where the conjoined tramways of the Hay and of the Kington Railways provided a pathway from the valley of the River Usk to the Radnorshire hills. There was a flow of coal and manufactured products towards Hay and Kington, whilst in the reverse direction there was a route for the carriage of limestone and lime, agricultural produce, the output of the iron foundry in Kington, and woollen goods. The tramway facilities encouraged the production of finished iron goods, and a new foundry was opened in 1820 by John Meredith, whose successful family business had already contributed much to the economy and prosperity of Kington, and whose successors would continue to do so.

For many years, and in their own way, the horse-drawn trams of the

Hay and Kington narrow gauge railways served their districts well, and, although traffic flows in each direction could be unequal and uneven, the lines were, from a commercial point of view, quietly successful. The heyday of the Kington Railway was the period from 1839 to 1845, when unspectacular but regular and reliable dividends of 3½ per cent were paid to the shareholders. Both the Hay and the Kington Railways became skilled in what would today be called 'yield management': they continually adjusted their 'tonnages' (charges) and 'drawbacks' (rebates) upwards and downwards so as to maximise revenue. Hence the income of the Kington Railway (often called 'The Road') was highly sensitive to the coal prices which could be achieved at Kington itself.

Proposals for Railways

During the 'Railway Mania' of the mid-1840s many long distance railways were proposed. Many such schemes were inherently impracticable, and, or, failed to attract sufficient support and firm promises of investment. Examples were proposals for railways between Worcester and West Wales and between Worcester and Cardigan Bay. A lesser plan to build a line between Leominster and Brecon via Hay also made no progress. Nevertheless, Leominster was to play an important part in the railway history of the area with which we are concerned. The town joined the railway network when it became an important intermediate station on a line built between Shrewsbury and Hereford.

The Shrewsbury and Hereford Railway

The Parliamentary session 1845 – 1846 signalled the culmination of the 'Railway Mania'. No fewer than 263 Bills authorising the construction of new railways were passed. Amongst them were those incorporating the Newport, Abergavenny and Hereford Railway (the NA&HR) and the Shrewsbury and Hereford Railway (the S&HR) companies. Both of the bills concerned received Royal Assent on 3rd August, 1846.

The Shrewsbury and Hereford Railway Act of 1846 authorised the creation of a capital of £800,000 (more than £73 million at 2022 prices). In the inevitable reaction which followed the 'Railway Mania' and in a time of more general economic decline, this sum was unattainable. Accordingly the project was simplified by limiting the new railway to a single line of rails, although (as was common in such cases) the bridges and earthworks were still to be made capable of accommodating double track if required at a later date; and by acquiring, for the relatively small sum of £12,000, the by now under-used Leominster Canal. The canal would be drained, and parts of its course for several miles north of Leominster could, as it was thought, be used for the new railway. In the event, however, little of the canal route was actually used by the S&HR.

The delays arising from financial and other difficulties meant that the time stipulated in the principal act for the construction of the line expired, but the powers were renewed in 1850 and then work started in earnest. The contractor was Thomas Brassey, who, in association with his partner William Field, offered to build the new line for the sum of £345,822, and for a specified time thereafter to work the line on behalf of the company. (Such an arrangement was common in the mid-Victorian period.)

The railway between Shrewsbury and Ludlow (27½ miles) was opened to traffic on 21st April, 1852. The more difficult section (23½ miles) between Ludlow and Hereford, which included Leominster and a tunnel (1,051 yards long) at Dinmore, was completed in the following year. The line was opened throughout to goods traffic on 30th July, 1853. Passenger services commenced on 6th December, in the same year, 1853, and ran from Shrewsbury to a temporary (and desolate) terminus just to the south of the later, and present, Barrs Court station on the *east* side of Hereford. Coming south, all S&HR trains could, from 1854, also run to Barton station, on the *west* side of Hereford, which was reached by the Newport, Hereford and Abergavenny Railway (the NH&AR) on 16th January, 1854. By means of this link between the S&HR and the NH&AR a through route between South Wales and Shrewsbury and beyond was established. One consequence (*inter alia*) of these developments was that coal and merchandise could be readily carried for long distances from both north and south to the town of Leominster.

From the outset, the S&HR was a success, and became the more so when, after the resolution of many problems between the two companies, through running with the NA&HR became possible by means of new junctions made on the north and west sides of Hereford. There was now continuous and direct rail communication between the Severn and the Mersey. Leominster greatly benefited from being served from both south and north, and from being connected with the national network, by which South Wales coal and many other forms of merchandise could be brought to this previously remote town.

The contract between Thomas Brassey and the S&HR came to its appointed end in 1862, whereupon the S&HR needed a new operator, since the company had no locomotives, rolling stock or other necessary resources of its own. The London and North Western Railway (LNWR) already possessed running powers over the NA&HR, and now offered to work the S&HR. The LNWR's own line between Shrewsbury and Crewe had opened on 1st September, 1858, and operation of the S&HR would allow the North Western to have continuous running between south-east Wales and the heart of its own system at Crewe.

The LNWR also invited the Great Western Railway (GWR) to enter a joint lease of the S&HR. The GWR was at first affronted by this offer and indeed opposed a Bill authorising the lease to the LNWR, but then realised that becoming a partner might enable it not only to restrain the North Western but also to extend its own domain westwards to the Welsh Border and beyond. Hence the GWR agreed to the proffered joint lease, another party to which was the West Midland Railway (WMR). This latter company had been formed on 1st July, 1860, by an amalgamation of the Oxford, Worcester and Wolverhampton Railway, the Newport, Abergavenny and Hereford Railway, and the (at that stage not yet complete) Worcester and Hereford Railway, which would form a bridge between the two larger concerns.

The three companies – the LNWR, the GWR and the WMR – became joint lessees of the S&HR in 1862. This arrangement was, however, in the event short lived, since on 1st August, 1863, the WMR was amalgamated with – in practice virtually absorbed by – the GWR, and from then on the LNWR and the GWR became co-equal lessees, and, from 1871, joint owners of the Shrewsbury and Hereford line. With a substantial increase in its portfolio of railways, including the lines of the WMR, and with the joint ownership of the S&HR, the GWR now had a powerful presence in the West Midlands and along the Welsh Border.

The Leominster and Kington Railway

It is now time to return to the development of the railway to Kington. The inhabitants of Kington had been disappointed in their desire for a connecting length of canal to be built between their town and the Leominster Canal, which at that time, it was still hoped, would run to Stourport-on-Severn, but which was in the event to remain permanently land-locked. Similarly, a plan formed in 1833 to construct a tramway along the course of the previously proposed canal route between Leominster and Kington did not proceed.

The fact that by late 1853 Leominster had become well placed on the railway map did, however, rekindle desires in Kington for a link with the new and then modern transport system. Accordingly plans were formulated for a standard gauge (4 feet 8½ inches) branch line, beginning from a junction just north of Leominster, and running along the plain of the River Lugg and then the valley of the River Arrow. These plans were developed by influential citizens of Kington and district, with the lead taken by William Bateman Bateman-Hanbury (1826 – 1901), the second Lord Bateman, of Shobdon Court. Baron Bateman was Deputy Lieutenant of Herefordshire until 1852, when he became Lord Lieutenant of the county, a distinction which he held for the rest of his life. He held the chairmanship of the Leominster and Kington Railway for 22 years.

The opening meeting to promote a new railway was held at Shobdon Court on 24th October, 1853, and was attended by local landowners, solicitors, and merchants; by Henry Robertson, engineer of the Shrewsbury and Hereford Railway; by William Field, a partner of the renowned railway contractor Thomas Brassey; and by David Wylie, who would become the engineer of the new Leominster and Kington

Shobdon Court near Leominster was built in the early 18th century by Sir James Bateman, Lord Mayor of London and Governor of the Bank of England, replacing a Jacobean house. After the death of the third Baron Bateman in 1931, who died without heir, the house was put up for sale. Still unsold two years later, Shobdon Court was demolished so its fixtures could be auctioned. *Oakwood Press*

company and later also that of the Kington and Eardisley Railway. It was resolved to seek Parliamentary authority for the construction of a line between Leominster and Kington at a cost estimated by David Wylie to be about £80,000.

Naturally, the development of these plans for a standard gauge railway between Leominster and Kington gave rise to concerns on the part of the Kington Railway (i.e. the tramway) proprietors, who foresaw, correctly, that a new railway as proposed would undermine, and perhaps even render obsolete, their long-established tramway service, and that it would in particular divert the all-important inwards coal traffic away from the lengthy and not very quick route via the canals and Brecon and Hay.

Accordingly, and led by one local landowner and major shareholder in the Kington Railway named James Davies (1777 – 1856), the tramway shareholders decided to petition Parliament about the Bill by which a newly-formed Leominster and Kington Railway Company (L&KR) sought statutory incorporation and powers to raise money and to construct the new railway. Their objections did not, however, prevail, and the Leominster and Kington Railway Act received Royal Assent on 10th July, 1854. The authorised capital was £80,000, and borrowing powers for £26,000 were also granted by the Act.

This measure neither required nor enabled the newly-incorporated company to acquire the Kington Railway. In 1856 the Kington Railway company made a direct appeal to the L&KR to purchase the old tramway. But the L&KR was not in a financial position to make such an acquisition, although it did accept that, as enjoined by the enabling Act, at Kington a 'junction' should be made between the tramway and the new railway. Such a 'junction' could not of course take the form of a convergence of tracks, since the tramway was a plate-way resting on stone blocks and of 3 feet 6 inches gauge, whereas the railway would be of 4 feet 8½ inches gauge and would be of conventional construction. In the event each concern built a siding close to the other's, thus providing a place of trans-shipment, where goods could be transferred between the two companies.

Construction of the Leominster and Kington Railway

The contract to construct the railway between Leominster and Kington was let to the experienced and respected firm of Brassey and Field, who, as we have seen, had built the important line between Shrewsbury and Hereford. The firm had offered (on 14th November, 1854) to construct the line for £70,000, to work the traffic over it until 30th June, 1862, and to pay the shareholders a dividend of 4 per cent annually.

Construction of the new line to Kington presented no particular difficulties, and no major earthworks, tunnels or viaducts were required. Work began in late 1854, when, on 30th November in that year, Lady Bateman turned the first sod at Kington, but at first progress was not rapid. The Chairman of the L&KR was Lord Bateman, who, as Lord Lieutenant of Herefordshire, was active and influential in county affairs. It may be surmised that he wished to obtain by agreement with his fellow landowners the land needed for railway purposes, and that he preferred not to alienate them by resorting to the powers of compulsory purchase which were contained in the enabling Act of Parliament. In response to gentlemanly negotiation, the necessary land acquisitions were gradually made, and in October, 1855, the railway reached Pembridge, 7 miles and 49 chains from the junction (Kington Junction) north of Leominster on the S&HR. Coal was delivered to the intermediate station at Kingsland on 24th December, 1855, and goods traffic to Pembridge began shortly afterwards.

By this time, the Company's funds were running low, and Brassey and Field (who already owned 25 per cent of the authorised initial share capital of £80,000) supplied a further £10,000 to be repaid at 5 per cent interest. This enabled work to proceed. The continuation of the line to Titley (11 miles and 48 chains from the junction with the S&HR) and to the terminus at Kington itself (13 miles and 25 chains) was completed by the midsummer of 1857. Hence, notwithstanding a gradual start, the line was completed within the (unusual) time limit of 3½ years stipulated by the Act. As was quite frequently the case with rural railways, the formation of the line and the overbridges and underbridges were made sufficiently wide to accommodate a double line of railway, but, except at the stations, the track from Kington Junction (Leominster) to Kington remained single throughout its existence.

Curiously, the proprietors and the contractors building the line between Leominster and Kington either overlooked or disregarded the provision in the Leominster and Kington Railway Act (10th July, 1854) which required the construction of a bridge to carry a road over the railway immediately to the east of Pembridge station. Instead, Messrs Brassey and Field built a level crossing. Naturally, this infraction did not escape the notice of Colonel Yolland, who, for the Board of Trade, inspected the line on Wednesday, 22nd July, 1857, and who, upon discovering the level crossing, was unable to recommend the opening of the line to passenger traffic.

This caused consternation, and an urgent meeting was held in London on Saturday, 25th July, when Lord Bateman, Mr Wylie and several directors met Lord Stanley of Alderley, the President of the Board of Trade. A gentlemen's agreement was reached, by which the L&KR directors promised to apply for a new Act to authorise (retrospectively) the level crossing, and were meanwhile permitted to hold the planned formal opening of the railway on Monday 27th July, but the general public had to await a further inspection (this time made by Captain Galton), and in the event were allowed to use the new line on and from Thursday, 20th August, 1857.

A measure to rectify the situation (the Leominster and Kington Railway Amendment Act) received Royal Assent on 19th April, 1859 (and became known as 'the Level Crossing Act'). In the long run, it would probably have been cheaper, and certainly more satisfactory, had the L&KR and the builders complied with the terms of the original Act. When, a few years later, the Hereford, Hay and Brecon Railway was built between Moorfields, on the west side of Hereford, and Three Cocks Junction, road overbridges for minor roads were built at Credenhill, Moorhampton and Kinnersley stations, and, although they incurred higher first costs, over time the bridges saved money as well as being inherently safer.

The line opens

The *Hereford Times* of Saturday, 1st August, 1857, contained a rapturous account of the celebratory opening held on the previous Monday, 27th July. Huge crowds had descended upon the elaborately decorated Leominster station, and a path had to be cloven through the surging masses to enable a procession of the privileged to gain access to the first official train to Kington. This train, the account continued, consisted of thirty or more carriages packed with passengers and was hauled by two locomotives, which were probably those belonging to Brassey and Field, the contractors who had built the line. Here, one fears, the writer has been a little carried away by excitement: it is scarcely conceivable that two small locomotives could haul thirty or more heavily-laden carriages up the long incline of 1 in 80 between

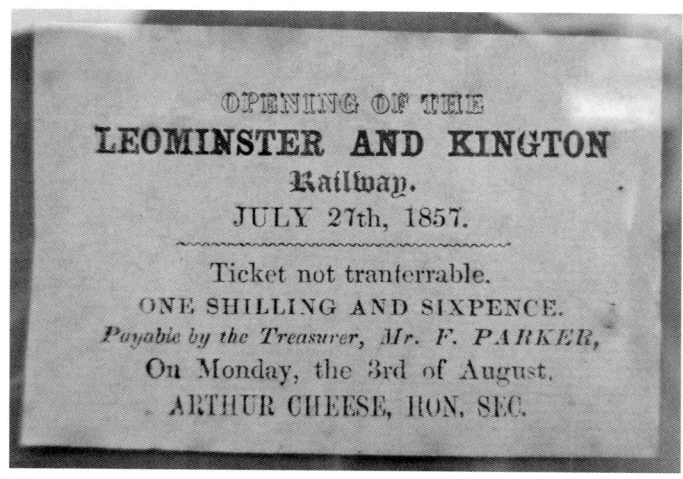

Ticket for the opening of the Leominster and Kington Railway.
© Andy Mabbett, in collection of Leominster Museum, 2023
This image is licensed under the Creative Commons Attribution-Share Alike 3.0 Unported licence.
to view the licence visit https://creativecommons.org/licenses/by-sa/3.0/deed.en

Pembridge and Titley, and still less so that they could control the descent of the train on its return journey down the same declivity.

Because of the late running of an important connection from the north, the 'monster train' left Leominster later than intended, but nevertheless received at Kington an ecstatic welcome, undampened by the rain which was by then falling. An interesting addition to the waiting and expectant throng was a party who had travelled from Hay, via the Hay and Kington Railways, in tramway wagons temporarily converted for passenger use. Other greetings came from further afield, from people who had travelled on horseback or in carriages from Builth Wells, Rhayader and Knighton. Some 300 participants repaired to the Oxford Arms, for a sumptuous meal hosted by Sir Thomas Hastings (whose wife Louisa Elizabeth inherited Titley Court), and followed by several speeches of mutual congratulation. The main party then returned by special train to Leominster, where, at the Royal Oak Hotel, Lord Bateman presided over a similarly lavish meal with further speeches.

After all this, the general opening of the line on Thursday, 20th August, 1857, may have seemed a slight anti-climax, but it was then that the daily life of the line began. The passenger service consisted of up to five trains daily between Leominster and Kington.

Kingsland station looking west towards Titley Junction. The size and nature of the buildings are remarkable for what was a wayside station.

John Alsop collection

Along the line

Stations had been built at Kingsland, Pembridge, Titley and Kington. The buildings at each of these places were surprisingly extensive, and each included a commodious station master's house as well as the more operational accommodation. In addition, a small private station was provided at Ox House (between Kingsland and Pembridge) to serve Shobdon Court. Usage of this private station may have been discontinued when the greater part of Shobdon Court was (intentionally) demolished in 1933, but it may have been intermittently and unofficially used during the Second World War by personnel proceeding to and from Shobdon airfield.

A passenger station (named Marston Road or Marston Lane) was also provided near Marston (between Pembridge and Titley) but this would seem to have been closed to passenger traffic in 1864. Much later, in 1929, a halt was built on or near the site of this station

Early years

In September, 1859, Thomas Brassey informed the L&KR directors that he was losing money on the operation of the line, and offered to pay a lump sum of £2,000 to terminate the contract. The directors, however, declined, and accordingly Brassey was obliged to continue to run the railway until the originally agreed end-date of 30th June, 1862. From 1st July in that year, operation of the L&KR was entrusted to the West Midland Railway (WMR). This company had been formed two years previously, in 1860, its constituents being the Oxford, Worcester and Wolverhampton Railway, the Newport, Abergavenny and Hereford Railway, and the Worcester and Hereford Railway (the last named being still partly incomplete at the time of the formation of the WMR). The terms with the owning company remained the same: the WMR would pay a guaranteed dividend of 4 per cent and a share of any further profits.

On 1st August, 1863, a little more than a year after it had succeeded Thomas Brassey in working the Kington line, the WMR itself was amalgamated with – in practice virtually absorbed by – the GWR, which thereupon took over the responsibility of running the L&KR. At first the GWR continued the financial arrangements made between the WMR

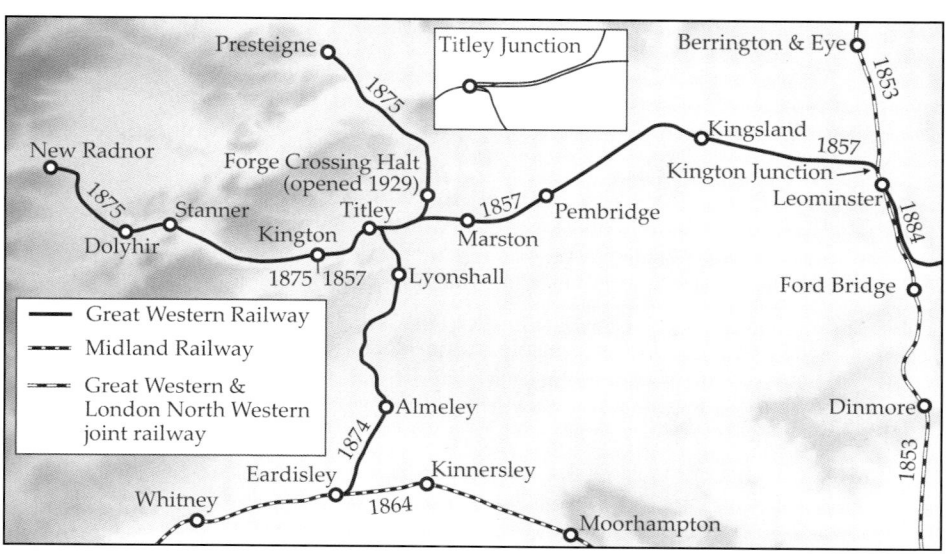

Map of the lines around Kington.
Relief shading contains OS data © Crown copyright and database right 2023.

and the L&KR, but after two years, and from 1st August, 1865, started to retain 60 per cent of the gross receipts (not only of the profits!) instead. In 1898 the GWR acquired the L&KR outright, and then the local company was dissolved.

The Hereford, Hay and Brecon Railway

During the mid-1850s various schemes were mooted for trunk railway connections between the West Midlands and West Wales. One such proposal would have encompassed Hereford and Brecon as staging posts along a line running between the West Midlands and the El Dorado of Milford Haven. In the absence, however, of firm financial support, this scheme, typically, flew forgotten as a dream at the opening day.

A practical plan

In 1857 Captain Walter Devereux of Tregoyd (the seat, near Glasbury, of Viscount Hereford) put forward a more modest and realistic plan for a local line to be built between Hereford, Hay and Brecon. This would partly run along the line of the Hay Railway (the tramway which ran between Brecon and Eardisley). Disappointed by an initial lack of support for his scheme, Devereux withdrew. Subsequently, however, the merits of his idea began to be appreciated, and plans were made for a Hereford, Hay and Brecon Railway (HH&BR). The promoters were greatly encouraged by the willingness of the proprietors of the Hay Railway to sell their tramway, and an agreement was sealed in November, 1859. By then Parliament had, on 8th August, 1959, passed the Hereford, Hay and Brecon Railway Act, which incorporated the company, made financial provisions and authorised the construction of the railway.

Opponents of the HH&BR rapidly acquired shares in the Hay Railway with a view to preventing the sale of the old tramway, but their attempts were unsuccessful: almost exactly a year after the passage of the principal Act, the Hay Railway Act of 6th August, 1860, gave effect to the agreement described above. Vesting took place on 22nd August, 1860, and the Hay Railway Company was finally wound up in 1862.

Naturally, the closure of the Hay Railway had serious consequences for the Kington Railway, for whom the route from and to the south was now permanently severed. The connecting line (at Eardisley) between the two tram roads had remained the property of the Hay Company, and so with the sale of the latter it became necessary for the Kington Railway to seek consent (which was forthcoming) from the HH&BR to use the link section in order to continue to gain access to the wharf at Eardisley and to reach the site of the future Eardisley station.

Tramway traffic between Kington and Eardisley was, however, light, and it became apparent that any future for the Kington Railway would lie mainly with its section between Kington and Burlingjobb, along which coal, the main commodity inwards, could be taken to the lime kilns at Dolyhir; and good quality limestone and the lime produced at Dolyhir could be taken to Kington for trans-shipment to the L&KR. (Lime is produced by heating limestone (calcium carbonate) to produce different kinds of lime (calcium oxide or calcium hydroxide), substances with many applications.) At this point we need to consider the slightly complicated history of the Kington and Eardisley Railway.

The Kington and Eardisley Railway

When it had become established that a standard gauge railway was to be built between Hereford, Hay and Brecon, the idea was formed that a similar railway could be built between Eardisley, which was to have a station on the new HH&BR, and Kington. This proposed new railway line would supersede the Kington Railway (i.e. the tramway), but, although it might be partly built upon the tramway formation, it would for the most part pursue a course further to the east.

In November, 1861, Mr W L Banks, who was the Secretary of the Hereford, Hay and Brecon Railway, offered (whether on his own behalf or on that of the HH&BR is unclear) to buy the shares of the Kington Railway: for each £100 share in the tramway, the holder could choose between £40 in cash, or £60 in shares in the proposed new company. Shortly afterwards, in December, 1861, the tramway shareholders were enticed by a slightly improved proposal made by Mr Thomas Savin, who also offered to issue £60 in shares but to pay £45 in cash for each Kington Railway share of £100. Mr Savin, who was an experienced engineer and entrepreneur, had gained high renown for his skills and achievements, especially in the realm of railway development, and he was now to act on behalf of the proponents of the Kington and Eardisley Railway (K&ER). On 19th April, 1862, the Kington Railway shareholders agreed that their tramway should be sold to the K&ER.

The way now lay clear, as it seemed, for the K&ER to take its next major step, that of obtaining Parliamentary approval. At this stage, the plan was to replace the tramway between Eardisley and Kington with a standard gauge railway, but to leave intact the Kington to Burlingjobb section. A chord would also be built from near Lyonshall (about 2½ miles east of Kington) to Marston on the L&KR, enabling trains to run from Eardisley (and hence from Brecon and South Wales) directly to Leominster and so to join the S&HR. This part of the plan – which would have brought additional traffic to the L&KR – excited, rather strangely, some opposition on the part of some (by no means all) of the L&KR shareholders and of Brassey and Field, who at that time were still operating the line which they had recently built. The Bill to give effect to the K&ER scheme was therefore opposed in Parliament, but the objections did not prevail, and the Kington and Eardisley Railway Act received Royal Assent on 30th June, 1862.

The newly-incorporated company was authorised to buy the Kington Railway, to build a standard gauge line from the tramway wharf in Kington to Eardisley and a branch between Lyonshall and the L&KR near Marston, to raise capital of £100,000 in shares, and to borrow up to £33,000, sums which seemed sufficient to construct what was in effect a quite simple connecting line between Kington and the HH&BR (and parts of which could withal be built upon an already existing formation). Payments to the Kington Railway shareholders were to be completed by 30th September, 1863, and any amounts still due after that date would attract 4 per cent interest from the K&ER. Thomas Price, who was the Clerk to the Kington Railway (and who held several other offices in the district) was to receive £50 per annum for life, in respect of loss of office.

If only the K&ER had been content with this outcome, the end result would have been more satisfactory, and certainly much quicker, than what actually transpired. As it was, however, Thomas Savin was eager to extend the line northwards, at first to Presteigne, and then, as he hoped, to Craven Arms and to the West Midlands, thus setting up a new, and major, route.

The first sod of the K&ER was cut at Kington by Lady Langdale of Eywood (near Titley) on Thursday, 12th March, 1863. Construction was, however, to proceed from the Eardisley (southern) end of the line. It was not to be expected that the course of a standard gauge line worked by steam locomotives and carrying passenger traffic would correspond exactly with that of a narrow gauge (3 feet 6 inches) tram road built for the carriage of wagons hauled by horses. Many adjustments were required, particularly in matters of levels and of curvature, and it has been calculated that in the event only about 2¼ miles of the new line fully utilised the formation of the tram road of the Kington Railway. This distance was mainly realised in a single section situated between Oldcastle and Lynhales.

Work on the new line had hardly started before the directors applied for, and obtained, Parliamentary sanction for an extension to Presteigne. The enabling legislation was the Kington and Eardisley Railway Act of 14th July, 1864, by which the company's share capital could be increased by £90,000 and the borrowing powers by £30,000. The directors now set their sights, and their hearts, upon further expansion northwards. They were encouraged by Thomas Savin, their adviser and contractor, who held out the possibility of an extension to Craven Arms and from there to the West Midlands.

In a 'Memorial' presented in November, 1864, some of the more cautious and sagacious shareholders of the K&ER company entreated the directors

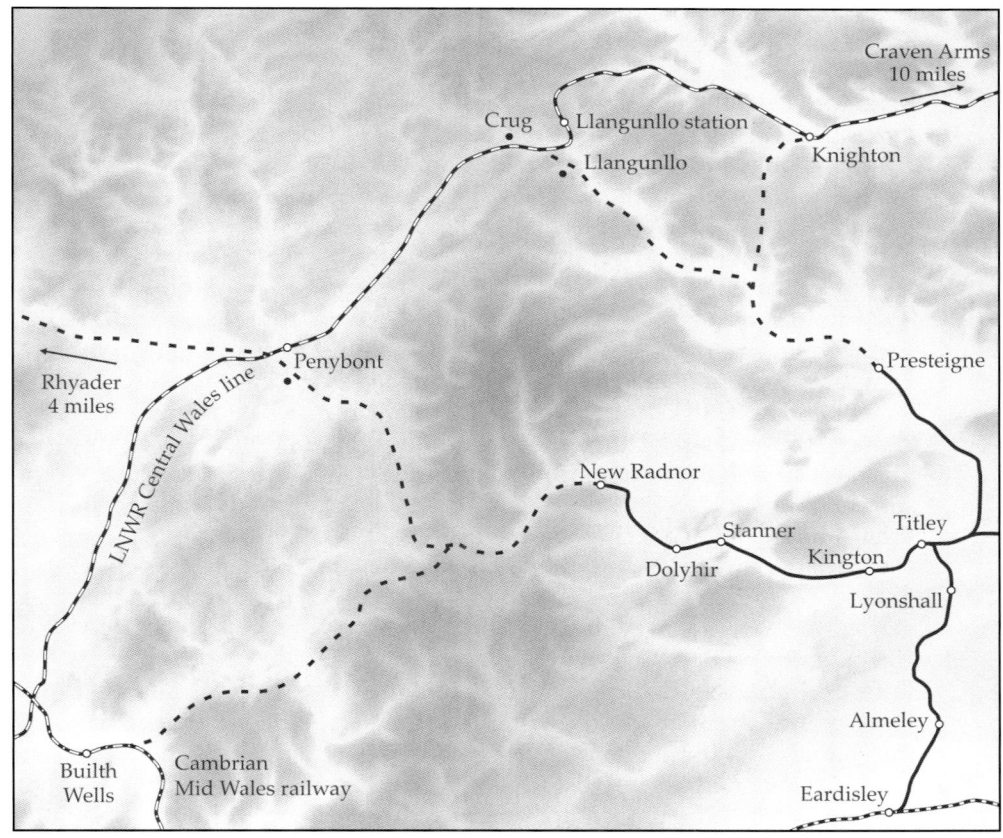

Onwards... the rough routes of proposed lines from Presteigne and New Radnor to the Central Wales and Mid Wales lines.

Relief shading contains OS data © Crown copyright and database right 2023.

to take a more realistic view of their enterprise and to restrict themselves to building the railway as envisaged by the enabling Acts of 1862 and of 1864 – that is to limit the line to a length between Eardisley and Presteigne only. This sensible advice went largely unheeded. An ambitious Bill (the Radnorshire Railways Bill) to link Presteigne with the Central Wales line at Knighton and (eventually) with the Cambrian Railways was withdrawn, but another Bill authorising a railway between Presteigne and a point west of Llangunllo (itself 6½ miles west of Knighton on the Central Wales Railway) was passed: this was the Lugg Valley Railway Act, which received Royal Assent on 29th June, 1865. Several other railways, including the Kington and Eardisley, the Leominster and Kington, the Central Wales and the Great Western Railways all agreed to afford running rights to this newcomer, which, however, was never built. Presteigne would almost certainly have benefited from being served by a through line, but, even so, was in the event perhaps fortunate at least in being served from 1875 onwards by a branch line built by the L&KR from Titley. For the time being, however, the directors of the K&ER, or at least some of them, remained enchanted by the idea of their railway running beyond Presteigne, but alas it never even reached that town, which was in due course to be served instead by a branch of the Leominster and Kington Railway.

By no means all of the capital authorised for the K&ER was actually forthcoming from investors, and, in an attempt to attract interest, the company obtained a further Act (25th May, 1865) authorising the conversion of £50,000 of the overall capital to 6 per cent preference shares. Unfortunately, this step failed to alter the situation to any appreciable extent. Local support, or at least local funding, was less forthcoming, and, with regret, perhaps also tinged with some relief, the Company at last decided not to proceed with the extension, and to revert to the earlier, and simpler, plan just to go to to Kington. Even so, however, progress on the ground was and remained slow, and a very serious development lay in store.

The early part of the year 1866 was a time of widespread financial failure, epitomised in the spectacular collapse of the bankers Overend, Gurney and Company – known as 'the bankers' bank' – which went into liquidation in June of that year. Many other companies, including other banks, failed, and the disaster bore especially hardly upon railway stocks. Thomas Savin, whose tentacular empire relied upon constant manipulation of credit and debt, was overwhelmed by the commitments arising from his manifold interests and activities, and his ensuing downfall led to personal bankruptcy.

After the loss of Savin, Thomas Evans of Newport became the contractor, but much remained to be done. An Act of 13th July, 1868, sanctioned some detailed changes to the plans, including further connections with the L&KR, but these were overtaken by the inevitable realisation that the extension to Presteigne and even the K&ER's own, separate, line into Kington had become unaffordable. The financial imperative was now for retrenchment.

Accordingly the directors took the painful decision to simplify the whole project, and to confine their line to a section leading from Eardisley to Titley, where a junction would be made with the existing L&KR, over whose metals the K&ER trains would gain access to Kington. Running powers over the L&KR between Titley and Kington had already been agreed, on 14th April, 1868, with that company and with the GWR. The distance between the junctions at Eardisley (the actual connection was 5 chains east of Eardisley station) and Titley was 6 miles and 72 chains. The effect of the numerous changes of plan and of the consequent needs for new legislation and for new capital had been to cause the many delays which attended the final, and simple, solution. The hapless K&ER did not even have its own line into Kington, and was dependent upon the use of the existing L&KR line.

The revised arrangements were authorised by the Kington and Eardisley Railway Act of 29th June, 1871. In 1872 Charles Chambers was engaged to complete the, still outstanding, northern, section to Titley, and by the summer of 1874 the line was at last finished. On Wednesday, 29th July, 1874, Colonel Hutchinson, on behalf of the Board of Trade, inspected the line between Titley and Eardisley, and approved it for use, subject to a minor change to the track layout at Almeley, one of the two intermediate stations on the line, the other being Lyonshall.

With their modest line at long last completed, the proprietors lost no time in opening it to the public, and on the following Monday, 3rd August, 1874, the first train departed at 12.20 pm from Kington to run to Eardisley, where a celebratory al fresco lunch was provided. On the return journey the passengers included Mr Justice Quain (1816 – 1876) and his retinue, who were using the new railway to cover a small part of their long journey to the Assizes at Presteigne.

From the outset, the train services were provided by the GWR, who had contributed a (not very munificent) loan of £5,100 towards the cost of constructing the line, and who would in due course (on 1st July, 1897) and in typical fashion cheaply acquire the line outright from the local company.

A Great Western Railway train for Kington waits to leave the up platform at Eardisley in 1909. The locomotive is 0-6-0 saddle tank No. 1137 of the Dean '1076' class.

Tony Harden collection

Eardisley

The line from Titley Junction joined the Hereford, Hay and Brecon line by means of a double trailing junction five chains east of the station itself, which comprised a passing loop, with side platforms, and several sidings. Therefore the K&ER trains entered the down (westbound) platform, and departed from the up (eastbound) platform (*see page 46*).

The New Radnor Extension

The K&ER was in effect the lineal successor of the Kington Railway, the tramway which ran, from an end-on junction with the Hay Railway at Eardisley, to Kington and so to the quarries and lime works at Burlingjobb. When the route and the function of the Hay Railway were largely taken over by the Hereford, Hay and Brecon Railway, the link with the Kington Railway at Eardisley was severed, and accordingly the Kington Railway could no longer form part of a transport corridor leading from Monmouthshire, Pontypool, Abergavenny and Brecon to the vale of the River Arrow and to the uplands of Radnorshire.

Moreover, the connection between Kington and Eardisley was now to be provided by the standard gauge railway, the K&ER, which was to take over not only the rôle of the tramway between those two places but also a portion of its formation. Any future for the Kington Railway therefore lay with the short remaining part of its system serving the quarries and lime works at Burlingjobb, and indeed the tramway continued to operate for those purposes. For its part, the K&ER (who had acquired the whole of the Kington Railway) could now contemplate the replacement by a standard gauge railway of the section of the Kington Railway lying between Kington itself and Burlingjobb, and then the extension of this (replacement) standard gauge railway as far as New Radnor, approximately 6½ miles from Kington: a temporary terminus at New Radnor could be seen as a staging post in a grand design for an – often mooted – new line running westwards to Rhayader or to Builth Wells and ultimately to the Cambrian coast at Aberystwyth. The gap between the northern end

A general view of New Radnor station and village. The station, seen in the foreground, is set some distance from the village, which is contained in a quite tight envelope. The never built continuation to Mid-Wales and the Cambrian Coast would have proceeded to the left.

John Alsop collection

of the K&ER at Titley and the commencement of the new line from Kington would have to be bridged by using the L&KR line between those two points.

Accordingly the directors of the K&ER in 1872 resolved to seek powers to build a new standard gauge railway from Kington, initially to New Radnor, from where, it was hoped, the line could later be extended as just described. A Bill to authorise the construction of the line to New Radnor and to make financial provisions received Royal Assent on 16th June, 1873 (the year before the Eardisley and Titley section opened). This K&ER Act enabled the company to raise an additional capital sum of £60,000, and increased its borrowing powers by £20,000. In the event still more money would be required, and a further Act, of 19th July, 1875, authorised another increase of £30,000 in capital and the raising of £10,000 by way of mortgage.

Alterations at Kington

Because of the existing road pattern and of the built environment in Kington, it was not possible to extend the railway beyond the 1857 terminus of the L&KR. The course of the new railway therefore necessitated a realignment at Kington. A new through station was built a short distance to the north of the original terminus of the L&KR, which now became a goods station and depot. West of Kington, the new railway followed the general, but not exact, course of the Kington Railway (i.e. the tramway) as far as Burlingjobb and the kilns at Dolyhir, the terminus of the tramway, and then of course broke new ground in the continuation to New Radnor, where, with a view to a further extension to Rhayader or to Builth Wells and so to the Cambrian coast, a through station, rather than a terminus, was provided. There were intermediate stations at Stanner and at Dolyhir, the latter being situated in the midst of the lime quarries and works. As often happened in such cases, the formation and bridges were built to accommodate double track, but only a single track was actually laid.

The contractor Charles Chambers, who was already engaged in completing the K&ER line south of Titley, was appointed to build the new line, and a contract was promptly signed on 23rd July, 1873. Work began quickly, but as usual there were some delays. It emerged that in practice some minor changes of the approved alignments and gradients were desirable, and Board of Trade approval for these was sought and was forthcoming.

HISTORICAL OUTLINE

The grassy platforms of the original (1857) terminus at Kington. After passenger traffic was transferred to the 'new' startion in 1875, the tracks here became the longest sidings in Kington goods yard. The station building is generally similar to that at Titley Junction.

John Alsop collection

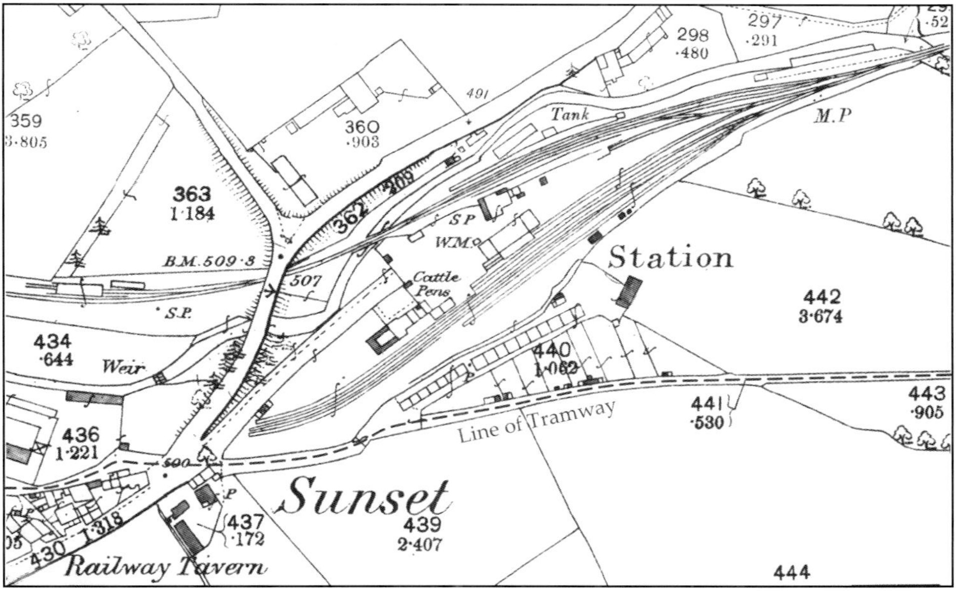

Kington stations 1886. The first station is in the centre of the map together with the cattle pens. Just to its north are the platforms of the second station, allowing through traffic.

© *National Library of Scotland, adapted and reduced from the 25 inch map, 2023.*
This image is licensed under the Creative Commons (CC-BY) licence.
to view the licence visit https://creativecommons.org/licenses/by/4.0/

On Friday, 6th August, 1875, Colonel Hutchinson inspected the New Radnor extension. In the main he reported favourably upon the new line, but drew attention to a few outstanding details. The principal stumbling block, however, was that 'arrangements have not yet been made as to its working, the owning company [the K&ER] having at present no rolling stock of their own'. He therefore concluded that in view of the 'incompleteness of the works and the absence of means for working ... the extension line could not be opened for passenger traffic without danger to the public'.

In retrospect, it seems surprising that this state of affairs had been allowed to arise. The inevitability of the GWR's working the line had, presumably, been apparent all along: that company had been working the L&KR since 1863, and had begun to work the Eardisley line in 1874, and no-one else had come forward to operate the extension. The K&ER board now hastened to make good the small shortcomings mentioned by the Inspector, and pressed the GWR to agree to run the line. The Board of Trade then accepted that the line could open for passenger traffic.

The extension from Kington to New Radnor was opened on Saturday, 25th September, 1875, with the accompaniment of the jubilant celebrations usual upon such occasions, in this case heightened by the – sadly never to be realised – prospect of a continuation of the line to the Cambrian Coast.

A charming posed photograph at New Radnor, as the train awaits departure for Kington and Leominster. *John Alsop collection*

The main building at New Radnor station was still not quite complete, but it was finished and ready for use soon afterwards. At first there were five trains daily in each direction between Kington and the new terminus, and this number was never surpassed. The line settled down to a quiet existence, and, as would be expected, the GWR in due course, on 1st July, 1897, acquired the assets. There was little recompense for the K&ER ordinary shareholders: each of their £100 shares was rewarded by the GWR with a payment of only £2.

The Presteigne Branch

At various times the K&ER proposed to extend its line to Presteigne . This line would have left the actually built K&ER at a point near Lyonshall and would have run northwards, intersecting the L&KR at Marston before continuing in a generally north-westerly direction to Presteigne. The K&ER Acts of 1864 and 1868 both envisaged such an extension, but the lack of enough financial support meant that this project was never realised. Indeed, the K&ER directors perhaps considered themselves fortunate in being able – at last and at least – in 1874 to complete their more modest and long delayed connecting line between Eardisley and Titley, where a junction was formed with the L&KR, over whose line to Kington the K&ER then used running powers on and from 3rd August, 1874.

Meanwhile, the L&KR had seen its own opportunity to reach Presteigne, and in an Act dated 31st July, 1871, had obtained powers to build a line, approximately 5¼ miles long, from Titley to the edge of the county town of Radnorshire. The Act authorised the L&KR to raise share capital of £40,000 and to borrow a further £13,000. On 24th July, 1871, a week before Royal Assent to the Act, the GWR agreed to work the line for 60 per cent of the gross receipts, an arrangement already applying to the main line of the L&KR between Leominster and Kington. On Thursday, 4th January, 1872, Miss Edith Green Price cut the first sod at Presteigne.

The line was built with a view to minimizing its first costs. It thus followed as far as possible the lie of the land, and its route entailed sharp curves and steep gradients. It may be doubted whether this policy brought about economies in the longer term, since more locomotive energy (requiring coal, water and oil) was needed to work the train service; more maintenance of the track was needed; and more general wear and tear arose.

The Presteigne branch ran eastwards and parallel with, but separate from, the L&KR line until the parting of the ways at a distance of approximately one mile east of Titley Junction. The branch then moved northwards, before taking up a generally north-westward course to the terminus at Presteigne. For most of the life of the station, the railway companies – including the Great Western – chose to spell the name 'Presteign'. On Saturday, 9th March, 1929, the GWR opened a halt named Forge Crossing Halt, situated at one 1 mile and 50 chains from Titley. There were no further stopping places between this halt and Presteigne station.

The location of the originally proposed terminus at Presteigne was considered to be inconvenient, and, with the consent of the Board of Trade, it was moved by some 32 chains to be nearer to the town centre. As at New Radnor, the station was arranged with a through layout, leaving open the possibility of a further extension, in this case from Presteigne to a junction with the Central Wales Railway. This addition never eventuated.

The Presteigne branch was built by Perry and Company of London, who were also the builders of the Royal Academy. The new line entailed

Attentive staff, and one young admirer, at Presteigne. Note that, as often occurred on GWR branch lines, the engine headlamp is placed just above the centre of the buffer beam, rather than in the more orthodox position below the chimney. *John Alsop collection*

many bridges, one of which (spanning the River Arrow) collapsed shortly after construction and was replaced by a more substantial structure. The line was inspected by Colonel Hutchinson on Thursday, 2nd September, 1875. He was quite satisfied (and even commented that some of the bridges seemed to have been made unnecessarily strong!). In the following week, on Thursday, 9th September, 1875, the line was opened to public traffic, with the accompaniment of festivities of surpassing excitement. From the outset, the branch was operated by the GWR. With the opening, just over two weeks later, on Saturday, 25th September, 1875, of the New Radnor extension, the Kington lines network was now complete. Between them, the L&KR and the K&ER had eclipsed the faithful old Kington Railway, but they proved to be welcome additions to the district.

By the summer of 1898 the whole of the Kington lines system was in the ownership of the Great Western Railway.

The Worcester, Bromyard and Leominster Railway

At this point we should consider another railway which had some bearing upon the development of the Kington lines, for the history of the Leominster and Kington Railway was connected with that of the line which ran to Leominster from Bransford Road Junction (previously called Leominster Junction), situated at 3 miles and 54 chains west of Worcester (Shrub Hill). In actuality this apparently simple cross-country line had a complex history: the original legislation authorising its construction dated from 1861, but it was not until 1897 that the entire route was completed. A detailed account of the chequered history of this line would lie outwith the present study, but the salient events and facts are as follows.

The Worcester, Bromyard and Leominster Railway Act received Royal Assent on 1st August, 1861, but, because of financial and contractual problems, the line was opened only in intermittent and protracted stages. Not until Saturday, 2nd May, 1874, was the line opened from Bransford Road Junction as far as Yearsett, a tiny settlement which was still some 3½ miles short of Bromyard. This temporary terminus was closed when, more than three years later, on Monday, 22nd October, 1877, the railway was at long last opened to Bromyard itself.

By then the original Worcester, Bromyard and Leominster Railway Company had, with a mixture of regret and relief, abandoned the idea

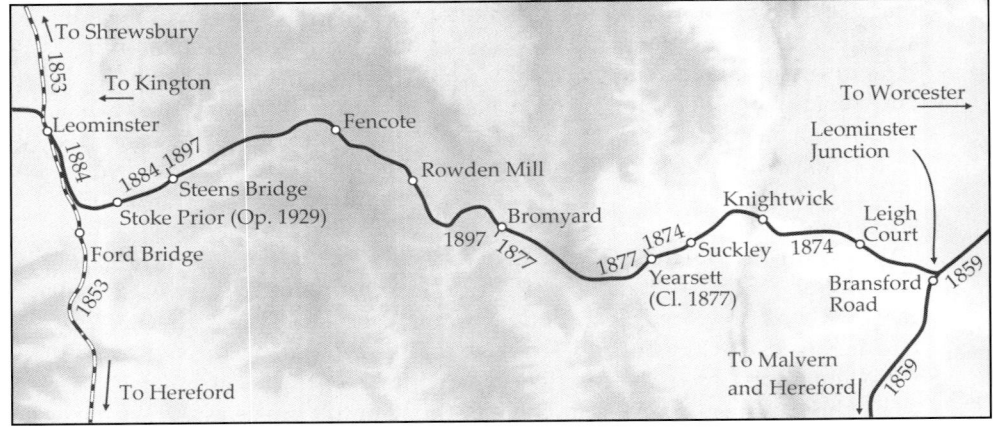

Worcester, Bromyard and Leominster Railway showing its route from Leominster Junction to the town.

Relief shading contains OS data © Crown copyright and database right 2023.

of the continuation of the railway through hilly and sparsely inhabited countryside from Bromyard to Leominster, but – in retrospect rather surprisingly – the completion of the original plan was taken up by a new concern, the Leominster and Bromyard Railway Company, which had been incorporated by an Act of Parliament passed on 30th July, 1874.

After repeated delays, the construction of this extension proceeded from the western (Leominster) end and was again prolonged. It was only on Saturday, 1st March, 1884, that the section of 3¾ miles between Leominster and Steens Bridge was opened to traffic, and then more than thirteen years elapsed before the remaining portion (9 miles) of the line between Steens Bridge and Bromyard was ready for opening on Wednesday, 1st September, 1897, more than 36 years after the original legislation for the construction of this modest cross-country line had been passed. Steens Bridge was not intended to be more than a wayside station and it was never a passing place for crossing trains. The loop was used for running round purposes during the station's use as a (long-lived) temporary terminus.

The relevance of this story to the Kington lines is that from the beginning of March, 1884, the Great Western Railway, which was already operating the lines to New Radnor, Eardisley (via Titley) and Presteigne, also assumed responsibility for providing the train service over the new section of railway between Leominster and Steens Bridge.

It gave effect to this by simply extending the journeys of certain Kington line trains to and from Steens Bridge, which for a long time remained the temporary terminus of the Leominster and Bromyard railway. On 1st July, 1888, and as expected, the GWR acquired the Leominster and Bromyard Railway, and the local company was vested in the Great Western Railway.

When, on Wednesday, 1st September, 1897, the intermediate section between Steens Bridge and Bromyard was at last opened, the GWR perpetuated the arrangement by which certain train services on the Kington lines were integrated with those running over the line running eastwards from Leominster – and which were now continuing to Bromyard and to Worcester. To the end, some of the passenger services over the Kington and New Radnor lines were operated by locomotives and rolling stock supplied by Worcester. Long 'dwell times' at Leominster did, however, tend to reduce the usefulness of the lengthy passage between the city of Worcester and the lonely terminus at the foot of the Radnorshire hills.

The Twentieth Century

In retrospect, the late Victorian age and the Edwardian era were the golden age of the Kington lines. The rural economy worked better for some people than for others, but in the aggregate this was a period of calm and tranquillity. The train service seems to have been attuned to the needs of this peaceable area of Herefordshire and of the Welsh Border. The prospect – if present at all – of mechanised road transport still seemed to be afar off.

The First World War ...

A few years later, the First World War (1914 – 1918) at first brought few outward changes to the railways of Britain as a whole. But as the war deepened, passenger services in particular were reduced all over the country, and towards the end of 1916 many were curtailed or withdrawn. The K&ER line between Titley and Eardisley was closed completely on 1st January, 1917, and the rails were lifted, ostensibly for use in France. Infrequent trains to Kington, New Radnor and Presteigne, did, however, continue to run.

... and its Aftermath

The war brought deep sorrows to many families and individuals. Afterwards, the longed-for peace did not of course bring about a reversion to pre-war conditions. The colossal waste of human life and of material resources was irreversible, and the countryside never quite recovered. On the railway, the numbers of passenger bookings fell after 1913, and after 1923 dropped steeply – so much so that by 1933 the numbers of tickets sold at some of the stations along the Kington line had fallen to less than a third of what they had been in 1903.

Under pressure from local interests, the GWR reluctantly reinstated the line between Titley and Eardisley. The opening of a sanatorium at Nieuport House, near Almeley, was, it was argued, deserving of rail access, and so was agricultural produce. The County Council held

Almeley station in August 1932, looking south to Eardisley. Opened in 1874, the station building is generally similar to those provided on the New Radnor extension, which opened in 1875. Beyond the station are the goods sidings, the points for which are worked from a ground frame housed in the hut in the distance on the right of the photograph.

John Alsop collection

that, in the long term, timber from its woodlands would also need to be conveyed by rail. Accordingly, the GWR reopened the line from Titley as far south as Almeley on Monday, 18th September, 1922 (although initially with only one train each way daily), and then all the way to Eardisley on Monday, 11th December in the same year.

Although at first falteringly, the motor bus gradually abstracted passenger traffic from the railway. Quiet railway stations pursued their timeless ways across the fields, far away from the villages and farms and steadings at which the motor bus could call at will. Further inroads to railway traffic were made by the establishment of a direct bus service between Kington and Hereford. The train journey entailed a change at Leominster, where there were sometimes inconveniently long waits for a connection; and, whereas the bus ran to the middle of the city, the railway station (Barr's Court) at Hereford was half a mile from the town centre.

Presteigne station looking south, August 1932. *John Alsop collection*

To its credit, in 1929 the GWR did make an effort to attract traffic by opening halts at Forge Crossing, on the Presteigne branch, on Saturday, 9th March, and at Marston, between Pembridge and Titley, on Friday, 26th April. The latter was on or near the site of the previous Marston Road (or Marston Lane) station which had closed, probably in 1864 (*see page 18*). The GWR also offered cheap fares for certain local events, and advertised occasional excursions, for example to the seaside, or to Windsor for a boat trip along a reach of the River Thames.

Few adjustments were, however, made to the train timetable itself or to marketing methods (or to the lack of them). In 1932, for example, the weekday passenger service between Leominster and Kington and New Radnor was substantially the same as it had been thirty years earlier, but the late Saturday evening service from Kington to New Radnor had by then been abolished, as had been the two return trains on Sundays. The services on each of the Eardisley and Presteigne branches had been reduced to three each way, and there was no augmentation on Wednesdays or Saturdays. The timings on these two branches had been adjusted so that services over both of them could be operated by a single train. Whether this ran at the times at which people actually wished to travel was another matter.

The 'Country Lorry' initiative

In rural areas generally, the inter-war period saw the rapid rise of local goods transport services provided by independent carriers using their own road vehicles, in some cases acquired cheaply from government surplus sources. Moreover, the railways were 'common carriers', which meant, broadly, that they were legally obliged to convey any goods which were presented to them, regardless of profitability, whereas most road transport operators could usually be selective, accepting only those loads which could be expected to be remunerative. In response to these tendencies, the GWR developed its own system of 'country lorries', whereby goods could be delivered to and collected from villages in the vicinity of an existing station, which would then become a railhead. For this purpose, Kington became 'a country lorry centre'. This system (which was adopted in many areas throughout the country) had some success in stemming the growth of road transport, but could not of course eliminate it.

The Second World War

The outbreak of war in September, 1939, did not initially bring changes to the Kington lines, but it could not fail to affect them. There was inevitably an increase in the movement of personnel and materials. Shortages of fuel oil impeded the use of road transport, whereas priority was given to the production of coal, which both enabled and required the railways to carry on.

Within a year of the beginning of hostilities the GWR took the opportunity to close completely, on Monday, 1st July, 1940, the Titley and Eardisley line. But the trains between Leominster and Kington continued to run, as did the already sparse services to Presteigne and to New Radnor. After the withdrawal of railway staff, the station at Stanner was, on and from Monday, 28th July, 1941, reclassified as a halt. The name-board on the platform was, however, never altered to display the changed status of this stopping place. Goods traffic at New Radnor saw a marked revival in one respect: timber from nearby Forestry Commission plantations which had matured between the wars needed to be conveyed, especially in order to provide pit props for use in the collieries of South Wales, where there was an urgent need for increased production.

A new, and sad, form of traffic was provided by the ambulance and other special trains which used the Leominster and Kington section to convey wounded and traumatised service personnel bound for the very large 107th and 122nd United States Army Hospitals which were established at Hergest, some two miles south-west of Kington (*see Chapter 2, page 53*).

Peace ... and Nationalisation

The ending of hostilities in 1945 led to a partial resumption of the state of affairs which had preceded the outbreak of war. But by now the connection to Eardisley had been lost; and road transport was again on the march. Modal shift from rail to road was, however, retarded by the maintenance of petrol rationing, which continued until 1950 (and which was briefly re-introduced at the time of the Suez Crisis in 1956), and this constraint had the effect of prolonging the usefulness of many secondary and branch railway lines, including those serving West Herefordshire and the Welsh Border.

On 1st January, 1948, nearly all of the railways of Britain were taken into public ownership, but of itself this nationalisation at first brought few alterations to services on the Kington lines, and the British Railways Western Region timetable operative from 27th September, 1948, was similar to the final GWR timetable.

The bleak opening of the year 1951 did, however, bring lasting change. Severe shortages of coal required the railways to effect operating economies, and all passenger services on the remaining Kington lines were suspended on and from Monday, 5th February, 1951. This meant that the last trains over the system ran on Saturday, 3rd February. Passenger trains began to run again between Leominster and Kington on Monday, 2nd April, 1951, but services to New Radnor and to Presteigne were never restored. Curiously, the Western Region public timetable for the summer of 1951 indicates passenger services on both the New Radnor extension and the Presteigne branch. The explanation for this inclusion may be that the timetable was compiled and printed before a final decision was taken not to reinstate the passenger services over the two sections concerned. The line between Dolyhir and New Radnor was closed completely on 31st December, 1951.

The resumed Leominster to Kington passenger service continued until early in 1955. It was finally withdrawn on and from Monday, 7th February, 1955, and, there being no Sunday services, the last scheduled service ran on Saturday, 5th February, 1955. The final workings – the 8.25 pm train from Leominster and the 9.05 return from Kington – consisted of an auto-train, coach no. 67 being in the care of 0-4-2 tank engine No. 1431. The 9.05 train normally ran as empty coaching stock, but on this occasion passengers were permitted to travel by it in order to return to Leominster.

For several years after the withdrawal of all passenger services, the line from Kington Junction to Dolyhir and the Presteigne branch remained open for freight traffic. A new connection was laid – at 10 miles and 46 chains from Kington Junction – between the Leominster and the Presteigne lines at the place where they diverged, and the point was hand-worked by the goods train crews. This alteration enabled the former Presteigne line track between there and Titley to be lifted, and also made it possible for the track layout at the former Titley Junction to be greatly simplified. The signal box there was closed in August, 1958.

Freight traffic to Dolyhir was discontinued on and from Monday, 9th June, 1958, but goods trains continued to serve the line as far as Kington and also the Presteigne branch. Traffic continued to dwindle, and the line between Leominster and Kington and the Presteigne branch were finally closed to all traffic on and from Monday, 28th September, 1964. This was also the day upon which the remaining goods train services over the HH&BR were withdrawn.

'The Kington Centenary Rail Tour'

In 1957, a special train was chartered by the Stephenson Locomotive Society, whose 'Kington Centenary Rail Tour' took place on Saturday, 27th July, precisely 100 years after the initial celebratory outward and return journeys of 27th July, 1857, between Leominster and Kington. The rail tour train consisted of two British Railways Western Region auto-coaches, numbered W242W and W243W, and was headed and propelled by auto-fitted locomotive no. 1455. It began its journey at Tenbury Wells and ran to Leominster, from where it went to Dolyhir (visiting en route the original terminus at Kington), and then reversed to Presteigne (by then so spelt on the station's name board). From there it proceeded to the 'new' (1875) station at Kington before returning to Leominster and terminating at Woofferton (the junction station for Tenbury Wells), from where participants made their own way home with the satisfaction, mingled with sadness, of having made their last ever passenger journeys over the Kington lines.

The Stephenson Locomotive Special Train of 27th July, 1957, with engine No. 1455 and auto coaches W242W and W243W, waits at Kington while participants converse with the engine crew and inspect the station. *Lens of Sutton Association*

An accident at Kington station. Probably on 11th March, 1914, when the Kington to Eardisley train on leaving the station was diverted from the running line into a siding where three horseboxes were standing. One passenger complained of being shaken and receiving bruises but there were no serious injuries. The line was damaged and it took several hours before it was cleared and repaired. *John Alsop collection*

Chapter Two

Operation of the Lines

Although Titley Junction was the pivot of the Kington lines, with routes radiating (in clockwise order) to Leominster, to Eardisley, to Kington (and so to New Radnor), and to Presteigne, it was, understandably, Kington which was the real node of the system, and (with the exception of the small number of trains which ran over the New Radnor extension) all services began and terminated at that town, which was much the most populated centre in the district. Motive power was provided by the depot at Leominster and by the sub-shed located at Kington itself; the layout at Kington included ample siding space for the stabling of rolling stock.

The railway between Leominster and Kington opened on Monday, 27th July, 1857, with the running of celebratory trains, and on Thursday, 20th August, in the same year public passenger services began. Next, after a long interval, was added the Kington and Eardisley line service, which commenced on Monday, 3rd August, 1874, with trains enjoying running powers over the L&KR line between Titley Junction and Kington. The pattern was completed by the opening of the Presteigne branch on Thursday, 9th September, 1875, and of the extension to New Radnor on Saturday, 25th September, 1875.

Gradients
From Leominster to New Radnor

Northwards from Leominster the main line rose at 1 in 400 towards Kington Junction (34 chains from Leominster station), and here the L&KR itself diverged to the west to follow the general course of the Pinsley Brook (which at its eastern end joined the Kenwater, a tributary of the River Lugg). The Pinsley Brook rose from a spring at Lady Pool, situated on Shobdon Marsh and about one mile east of Pembridge station. Consequently the gradients along this section were in the main quite slight, and, with a few short exceptions, did not exceed 1 in 310 all the way to the source of the brook. From there the railway rose at 1 in 206/207 both before and after Pembridge station; the line was then level for rather more than half of a mile before encountering a relatively steep rise at 1 in 106 to Marston. It then rose much more steeply, at 1 in 80, to a summit just before Titley, through which the line descended at 1 in 132 to a slight dip, after which it rose at varying gradients, none of them steeper than 1 in 132, to Kington.

Beyond Kington the railway rose continuously and at very rapidly changing inclinations, some as steep as 1 in 60, to a point just before New Radnor station, which itself was situated on level track. Many of these steeper and frequently altering pitches reflected the course of the original Kington Railway (the tramway) on its way to Burlingjobb.

From Titley to Eardisley

Upon leaving Titley, the K&ER rose at continually altering and often steep gradients to the second highest point on the route to Eardisley. For a distance of more than a quarter of a mile, the inclination upwards was at 1 in 50. There followed brief downhill, uphill, and again downhill sections through Lyonshall station until the line ascended again at 1 in 50 to the summit, three miles from Titley. Stop boards were provided at 36 chains from Titley to direct the pinning down of brakes on unfitted vehicles preparatory to the descent to the junction; and at 3 miles and 1 chain from Titley for the same purpose on trains about to descend to Eardisley.

Beyond the summit the railway descended almost continuously, past Almeley station, all the way to Eardisley in the broad Wye Valley. There was a brief level section, but otherwise the downward gradients were steep, with several lengths at inclinations varying between 1 in 47 and 1 in 44. This headlong descent ended when the line met the more evenly graded HH&BR line at Eardisley Junction signal box, 5 chains east of Eardisley station.

From Titley to Presteigne

The branch line to Presteigne ran next to the L&KR line to a point (where until 1958 there was no physical connection between the two lines) about one mile east of Titley. Hence the Presteigne line fell at 1 in 80 before it parted from the Leominster line. It then followed the lie of the land, resulting in a switchback of gradients, the steeper of which included pitches of between 1 in 45 and 1 in 53. Presteigne station itself was situated on a rising gradient of 1 in 239 towards the buffer stops.

Passenger train services

The early years of the 20th century saw what was perhaps the most intensive service of passenger trains upon the Kington lines. Although Titley was the junction for all four lines – to Leominster, Eardisley, Kington and Presteigne – it was Kington which was the hub of the system. This was natural, for the town was the largest of the settlements served by the railway. In 1851 the population had been 1,939, and by 1881 had risen by just over one thousand to 2,952. Thereafter the population sharply declined, to 1,688 in 1921, and then gradually rose to 1,890 in 1951, at the beginning of the decade in which the lines closed to passenger traffic.

In 1902, for example, there were six passenger trains running from Leominster to Kington; and of these three continued to New Radnor. In the reverse direction three started from New Radnor, and two from Kington. Perhaps a little unexpectedly a late evening service ran from Kington to New Radnor and back on Saturdays. There were four trains each way over each of the Eardisley and Presteigne branches, with a

The heyday of the Kington lines. This is the timetable for January to April, 1902. The Kington and New Radnor line enjoys a good service, and the branches to Eardisley and to Presteigne have four trains daily in each direction. Moreover, the Presteigne line has an additional early evening train on Wednesdays and Saturdays.

LEOMINSTER, KINGTON AND NEW RADNOR. (Week Days only.)

Miles			a.m.	a.m.		p.m.	p.m.	p.m.	p.m.			a.m.	a.m.	p.m.		p.m.	p.m.	p.m.
...	Leominster ...... dep		6 18	9 52	...	12 42	5 0	6 0	9 5	New Radnor ...... dep	...	10 50	...	...		2 30	6 5	...
4¼	Kingsland . . . . . . "		6 28	10 1	.	12 54	5 9	6 9	9 14	Dolyhir . . . . "	...	10 56	.	.		2 36	6 11	.
8	Pembridge . . . . . . "		6 37	10 9	...	1 5	5 17	6 17	9 22	Stanner . . . . "	...	11 0	.	.		2 40	6 15	.
10	Marston Halt . . . "		.	10 14	.	1 11	5 22	6 22	9 28	Kington . { arr	7 22	11 6		.		2 46	6 21	.
12	Titley . . . . "		6 51	10 21	...	1 17	5 28	6 30	9 35	. dep	7 22	11 10	1 40	.		2 53	6 27	7 40
13½	Kington . . { arr		6 56	10 24	...	1 23	5 32	6 35	9 39	Titley . . . . "	7 25	11 14	1 45	.	Saturdays only	2 56	6 31	7 44
	dep		—	10 28		1 55	5 38	—		Marston Halt . . . "	7 30	11 19	1 49	.		3 2	6 37	7 49
16⅞	Stanner . . . . "		...	10 35		2 3	5 45		.	Pembridge . . . . . "	7 36	11 24	1 55	.		3 8	6 42	7 55
17⅞	Dolyhir . . . . "		...	10 39		2 7	5 49	...	.	Kingsland . . . . . "	7 44	11 32	2 5	.		3 18	6 52	8 4
20⅞	New Radnor . . . arr		.	10 45		2 13	5 55	.	.	Leominster . . . . arr	7 54	11 41	2 15	.		3 28	7 0	8 14

KINGTON AND PRESTEIGN. (Week Days only.)

Miles			a.m.		p.m.		p.m.				a.m.		p.m.		p.m.
...	Kington . . . . . . dep		10 25	...	1 15	.	5 23	...	Presteign . . . . . . dep		10 48	...	2 38	.	6 3
1½	Titley . . . { arr		10 29	.	1 18	.	5 26	.	Forge Crossing Halt . . "		10 55	.	2 46	.	6 13
	dep		10 30	.	1 22	.	5 31	.	Titley . . . . { arr		11 0	.	2 54	.	6 19
3½	Forge Crossing Halt . . "		10 33		1 26	.	5 35	.	dep		11 1	.	2 58	.	6 20
7¼	Presteign . . . . . . arr		10 42	.	1 36	.	5 48	.	Kington . . . . . . arr		11 5	.	3 2	.	6 24

KINGTON AND EARDISLEY. (Week Days only.)

Miles			a.m.		a.m.		p.m.				a.m.		n'on		p.m.
...	Kington . . . . . . dep		9 0	...	11 16	...	3 30	...	Eardisley . . . . . . dep		9 57	...	12 0	...	4 48
1½	Titley . . . . "		9 5	.	11 21	.	3 35	.	Almeley . . . . . . "		10 2	.	12 6	.	4 53
3½	Lyonshall . . . . . . "		9 10	.	11 25	.	3 40	.	Lyonshall . . . . . . "		10 10	.	12 15	.	5 1
6½	Almeley . . . . . . "		9 25	.	11 34	.	3 55	.	Titley . . . . "		10 15	.	12 22	.	5 6
8½	Eardisley . . . . . arr		9 38	.	11 39	.	4 5	.	Kington . . . . . . arr		10 18	.	12 26	.	5 9

Thirty years on, the 1932 timetable indicates some small reductions. There are no longer any Sunday trains. The branches to Presteigne and to Eardisley now have only three services each way daily, and are timed so that they can be operated by a single train.

fifth, evening, return service over the latter on Wednesdays and Saturdays. So on most weekdays, there were no fewer than 27 passenger train movements between Kington and Titley Junction, and this figure rose to 29 on Wednesdays and Saturdays.

On Sundays an early morning mixed train left Leominster at 5.30 am, and at 6.10 arrived at Kington, from where it returned at 8.00. It would seem that this train was provided primarily for the collection of milk traffic. On Sunday evenings a passenger train departed from Leominster at 6.40 pm, and arrived at Kington at 7.15, the return journey beginning at 7.45 and reaching Leominster at 8.20. (A journey time of 35 minutes was standard for passenger trains between the two towns.) Normally no Sunday trains ran on the branches to Eardisley, to Presteigne or to New Radnor.

Eardisley

The Kington and Eardisley Railway (K&ER) opened on Monday, 3rd August, 1874, that is, in the year in which the Midland Railway (MR) took a lease of the Hereford, Hay and Brecon Railway (HH&BR)

between Hereford (Moorfields) and Three Cocks Junction. The MR had been operating the HH&BR since 1st October, 1869.

The K&ER was operated, but not yet owned, by the Great Western Railway, which had previously (and literally) placed obstacles in the way of the Midland Railway's use of Barton station in Hereford. The Midland seems now not to have been particularly accommodating towards the new entrant at Eardisley, where the station was a crossing place on the single line between Hereford and Three Cocks Junction. There was a platform on each side of the crossing loop, and it would, theoretically, have been possible to convert the up (Hereford bound) platform into an island on railway-owned land in order to provide a bay for the Kington line trains. In the event, however, the Midland Railway built a substantial brick goods shed there and GWR trains had to use the side platforms and to retire to a siding if, as sometimes happened, the crossing loop was needed for HH&BR line trains to pass or to overtake one another.

This subordination of the GWR trains persisted in the period of the Grouping. In the summer of 1938, for example, the morning train from Hereford to Brecon (the return working of the 6.50 am from Brecon) departed from Barrs Court at 9.25 am and was booked to call at Eardisley and to leave there at 10.00. At Eardisley it met the GWR train which had set out from Kington at 9.00 am, and which, after calling at all stations, had arrived at the junction at 9.38.

The timetable in Bradshaw's Guide for July, 1938, is generally similar to the 1932 version, but an interesting difference is that there is now a late evening train, on Saturdays only, between Leominster and Kington.

Passengers and parcels were exchanged, and, 2 minutes after the Brecon bound train had left, the GWR train departed at 10.02 to return to Kington.

On Wednesdays (market day in Hereford), however, an additional 8.50 train from Brecon was booked to cross the other two trains at Eardisley, and to depart from there at 9.59. Since both platform lines would thus be required for HH&BR trains, the GWR train would have to be (literally!) sidelined and to take refuge in a siding to the west of the station. This made it impossible – especially if the 8.50 train from Brecon was running late – for the GWR train to leave punctually at 10.02, and to arrive on time at Titley, where it was due to call from 10.17 to 10.18, and at Kington, where it was due to terminate at 10.22. Late running of the 8.50 train from Brecon had inevitable consequences for the 9.52 passenger train from Leominster to New Radnor which was due to follow closely the branch train from Eardisley, and to call at Titley at 10.22 and to arrive at Kington at 10.26, at either of which places passengers from the Eardisley line could change into the ex-Leominster train if they wished to travel beyond Kington. This delayed ex-Leominster train had no opportunity to make up time at New Radnor, where it was due to arrive at 10.45 and to depart again for Leominster at 10.50. Thus it was allowed only five minutes there (see below) while

An eastbound train awaits departure from the down platform at Kington. Note the arched waiting room upon the up platform, and the tall water tower beyond.

Lens of Sutton Association

station business was performed and while the engine ran round the train and carried out the necessary brake test. A late departure from New Radnor could thus result in a late arrival at Leominster (due 11.41), and hence ran the risk of missing a connection at 11.50 with a southbound train for Hereford and for other destinations as far away as Penzance. Such could be the consequences of the lack of facilities at a remote country junction!

Although the K&ER was not a long railway (the distance between the junction at Titley and that with the HH&BR just east of Eardisley station was 6 miles and 72 chains), punctuality was not a strong point, with the result that there were delays to HH&BR trains and missed connections. Some slow journeys along the K&ER were occasioned by the fact that the trains concerned were mixed, and the 'dwell times' at Lyonshall and at Almeley were prolonged as vans and wagons were attached and detached or loaded and unloaded.

Passenger rolling stock

Neither the L&KR nor the K&ER owned passenger rolling stock, and hence the coaches (or 'carriages') were supplied by the operators: first by the contractors Brassey and Field; then by the West Midland Railway; and after this by the Great Western Railway, which in any case acquired the two local companies in 1898 and in 1897 respectively. For many years the passenger trains consisted of three or four four-wheeled coaches, and these were gradually succeeded by four coach sets of six-wheeled stock, the coaches comprising a brake third, a composite, an all third, and a van.

After the First World War bogie coaches began to appear. These were in the main 'cascaded' from main lines, and some had clerestory roofs. In the 1930s the line from Leominster to New Radnor saw the introduction of some of the then modern 'B' sets. These were close-coupled pairs of non-corridor compartment coaches designed for use primarily on suburban lines but also on some branch lines, especially in the west of England. Each coach had a brake end for a guard, and six compartments, one of which was suitably sized and upholstered for first class travel. The Worcester Division received a small allocation of these coaches, and that is how they came to be used on the Kington lines, reaching Leominster via the Bromyard line. In the late 1930s accommodation on the Eardisley and Presteigne lines began to be provided by a single modern non-corridor composite bogie coach, to

No. 12.

LEOMINSTER, KINGTON AND NEW RADNOR, PRESTEIGN AND EARDISLEY BRANCHES.

Leominster and Kington Single Line Worked by Electric Train Staff between Kington Junction (Leominster) and Kington

Kington and New Radnor Single Line worked by Wooden Train Staff, and only one Engine in steam at a time (or two or more coupled together) between Kington and New Radnor.

Crossing Stations.—Kington Junction, Pembridge, Titley and Kington. All Trains must stop at Kington. *Two Passenger Trains conveying Passengers must not under ordinary circumstances cross at Pembridge.*

Titley & Presteign and **Titley & Eardisley** Single Line worked by Train Staff, and only one Engine in steam at a time, or two or more coupled together.

DOWN TRAINS.—WEEK DAYS ONLY.

M.P. Mileage from Kington Jct.	Miles	Miles	STATIONS	Station No.	Gradient	Time allowances for Ordinary Freight Trains. See page 2.			B Mxd.	B Pass.	B Goods arr.	B Goods dep.	K Pass. dep.
M. C.	M C.	M C.				P. to Point times. mins.	Allow for start. mins.	Allow for stop mins.	A.M.	A.M.	A.M.	A.M.	A.M.
—	—	—	**Leominster** dep.	4601	—	—	—	—	6 18	9 52	—	8 5	...
—	—	—	Kington Jct. ,,	4600	—	2	—	—	CS	CS	C S		...
3 72	—	—	Kingsland ,,	4622	176 R	9	1	1	5 29	10 1	8 17	8 55	
7 49	—	—	Pembridge ,,	4623	208 R	9	1	1	6 38	10 9	9 5	9 30	
9 34	—	—	Marston Siding ,,	4624	106 R				—	10 15			
9 40	—	—	Marston Halt ,,		106 R								
34 chs. Leominster to Kington Junction.	2 21	—	**Eardisley** dep.	4628	—				..	..			10 2
	5 38	—	Almeley ,,	4627	126 R				..	..	RR between Dolyhir and New Radnor		10 7
	6 46	—	Lyonshall ,,	4626	44 R				..	..			10 14
	—	—	Stop Board ,,						..	..			
	—	4 7	**Presteign** dep.	4634	—				..	..			—
	—	—	Forge Cross'g ,,		—				..	..			—
11 48	7 2	5 57	Titley { arr.		47 R				6 51	10 21			10 18
			{ dep.	4625	80 R	12	1	1	6 52	10 23	C R		10 19
			{ arr.						6 56	10X26	10 5	11X15	10X22
13 28	8 62	7 37	**Kington** { dep.	4629	132 R	14	1	1		10 28			
16 18	—	—	Stanner ,,	4631	60 R	12	1	1		10 35	C R		
17 32	—	—	Dolyhir ,,	4632	66 R	5	1	1		10 39	11 30	12 0	
19 66	—	—	**New Radnor** arr.	4633	50 R	6	1	1		10 45	12 7	—	

STATIONS	B Pass.	a Mixed	a	B Mixed	B	K Goods N	K Goods	B Goods	B Pass.	b Mixed	B Pass.	B Pass. SX	B Pass. SO
		arr. dep.	dep.	arr. dep.	dep.	dep.	dep.	dep.	dep.	dep.	dep.	dep.	dep.
	A.M.	P.M. P.M.	P.M.	P.M. P.M.	P.M.	P.M.	P.M.	P.M.	P.M.	P.M.	P.M.	P.M.	P.M.
Leominster dep.	....	Runs Tues.	noon	— 1238	1 35	RR	...	...	5 0	—	6 0	9 5	10 8
Kington Junc ,,	..	as per	Tuesdays only.	CS	CS	CS	SX	...	CS	...	CS	CS	CS
Kingsland ,,	...	next Col.		12 48 12 53	CS	...	RR	...	5 9	—	6 9	9 14	10 17
Pembridge ,,	...	...		1 1 1 3	CxS	M	...	...	5 17	...	6X17	9 22	10 25
Marston Sdg ,,	...	...		... ...	...	...	...	...	...	...	...	...	...
Marston Halt ,,	...	...		1 9 1 10	—	...	...	...	5 23	...	6 23	9Q30	10Q 35
Eardisley dep.	...	12 5	12 0	...	...	...	...	448	...	...	...	...	...
Almeley ,,	...	12 11 12 17	12 6	...	...	2 25	...	4 53	...	...	...	...	...
Lyonshall ,,	...	12 25 12 33	1215	...	...	2 50	...	5 1	...	...	...	...	...
Stop Board ,,	...			...	...	2 57	...	...	...	...	...	...	...
Presteign dep.	10 51	...	...	...	...	238	2 40	...	...	6 3	...	...	...
Forge Cr'g ,,	11 0	...	...	...	...	2 49	...	...	...	6 14	...	...	...
Titley { arr.	11 3	12 39	12 41	1221	...	3 0 2 54	CS	5	5X29	6 19	6X29	9 37	10 40
{ dep.	11 4	—	—	1222	1 17 X1 20	CS	3 9 2X58	—	5 30	6 20	6 32	9 38	10 41
Kington { arr.	11 7	1246	—	1226	1X24 1 55	2X10	3 15 3 2	5 0 5	9 5 33	6X24 635	941	10 44
{ dep.								5 38					
Stanner ,,	...	...	...	...	2 3	...	...	5 45	...	...	...	...	...
Dolyhir ,,	...	...	...	...	2 7	...	...	5 49	...	...	...	...	...
New Radnor arr.	...	...	...	...	2 13	...	...	5 55	...	...	...	...	...

M—Lyonshall arrive 2.37 p.m.   N—Runs on Kington and Presteign Cattle Sale days.
Q—Arrive 9.27 p.m. (10.30 SO).   Time allowed for Guard to extinguish lamps when necessary.

6.18 a.m. (Mixed) Leominster to Kington.
To be so formed as to avoid the necessity of an assistant Guard from Leominster. The Passenger Brake third must be formed next in front of the Guard's Van and be used for Mails only, under the control of the Guard.

12.38 p.m. Mixed Train Leominster to New Radnor.
1. As far as possible the Roadside Vans must be sent from Leominster by the 8.20 a.m. Goods Train.
2. When, however, any miss that train, if only the London and Kington Roadside only, the 12.38 p.m. ex Leominster it will be marshalled behind the rear Van and be transferred to the 1.22 p.m. ex Titley to Presteign. Presteign will unload their goods and return the van to Kington by 2.38 p.m. In this case Kingsland, Pembridge and Titley will take out their goods.
3. When two or more Roadside Trucks are sent with 12.38 p.m. ex Leominster they will be marshalled behind the passenger train with a four wheel passenger van in rear and all will be taken through to Kington. Kington will then send the Titley, Pembridge, and Kingsland goods back by the 1.50 p.m. Goods Train, the Presteign by the 5.23 p.m. Passenger Train, the New Radnor by the 5.38 p.m. Passenger Train. Every effort must be made to work the 12.38 p.m. Leominster to Kington punctually and the 2.38 p.m. ex Presteign must leave to time.

An extract from Section 12 of the GWR 'Service' (Working) Time Table current from 6th July, 1936, to 27th September, 1936. The timings on the Presteigne and Eardisley branches have been arranged so that all services could be operated by a single train. The cumbersome

No. 12.

LEOMINSTER, KINGTON AND NEW RADNOR, PRESTEIGN AND EARDISLEY BRANCHES.

UP TRAINS.—WEEK DAYS ONLY.

Miles. M C	Miles. M C	Miles. M C	STATIONS.	Station No.	Grad-ient.	Time Allow. for Ord'ry Freight Trains. See p. 2 P. to P. times	All w for Stop.	All w for Start	B Mixed. arr.	B Mixed. dep.	B Pass.	B Pass.	B Pass.	K Goods. arr.	K Goods. dep.
						Min	Min	Min	A.M.	A.M.	A.M.	A.M.	A.M.	P.M.	P.M.
			New Radnor dep.	4633	—			1	..	..	..	..	10 50	..	..
1 71			Stop Board ,,	—	50 F	4	1	1	..	..	..	..	..	..	R R
2 39			Dolyhir ,,	4632	50 F	2	1	1	..	..	..	10 56	..	R S	R X
3 53			Stanner ,,	4631	66 F	3	1	1	..	..	..	11 0	..		
5 45			Stop Board ,,	—	150 F	4	1	1	..	..	..	..	..		
6 43			**Kington** arr.	—	—				..	..	..	11 6	..		
			dep.	4629	60 F	3	1	1	7 21	..	9 0	10×29	11×10	11 17	..
8 23	1 60	1 60	Titley arr.	—	—	4	1	1	7 25	..	..	10 32	11×13	11×20	1 30
			dep.	4625	132 R				7 26	9 4	9 5	10 33	11 14	11 22	..
	3 30		Forge Cross'g dep.	—	—				..	..	..	10 36	..	..	..
	7 37		**Presteign** arr.	4634	—				..	..	..	10 45	..	..	..
3 24		3 24	Lyonshall dep.	4626	50 R				..	9 9	9 15	..	..	11 26	1 40 1 50
4 61		4 61	Stop Board ,,	—	—				..	..	..	..	..	156	P 1 58
6 41		6 41	Almeley ,,	4627	44 F				..	9 24	9 32	..	..	11 34	2 5
8 62		8 62	**Eardisley** arr.	4628	126 F				..	9 38	..	..	..	11 39	—
			Marston Halt dep.	—	—				7 32	..	..	..	11 20	..	..
10 36			Marston Siding ,,	4624	80 F				..	..	..	..	..	..	..
12 22			Pembridge ,,	4623	106 F	10	1	1	7 37	..	..	..	11 25	..	..
15 79			Kingsland ,,	4622	208 F	9	1	1	7 46	..	..	..	11 34	..	..
19 71			Kington Junc. ,,	4600	176 F	9			CS	..	..	..	CS	..	..
20 25			**Leominster** arr.	4601	—	2	1		7 55	..	..	..	11 41	..	..

STATIONS.	B Pass. dep.	B Mixed.	B	K Goods. arr.	K Goods. dep.	B Pass.	B Goods.	B Mixed. arr.	B Mixed. dep.	K Goods. arr.	K Goods. dep.	B Cattle	B Pass.	B Mxd.
	P.M.	P.M.	P.M.	P.M.	P.M.	P.M.	P.M.	P.M.	P.M.	P.M.	P.M.		P.M.	P.M.
New Radnor dep.		..	..	—	12 25	2 30	..	..	..	..	..		6 5	..
Stop Board ,,	SO	..	..	12 30 P	12 32	..	RR	..	..	..	V		..	..
Dolyhir ,,		..	..	12 35	12 45	2 36	..	..	..	..	..		6 11	..
Stanner ,,		..	..	12 50	R 1 0	2 40	..	..	..	..	W		6 15	..
Stop Board ,,	SO	..	..	1 8	P 1 11	..	..	..	..	..	..		..	..
Kington arr.		..	..	1 15	X	2 46	..	..	..	..	..		6 21	..
dep.	1 15	1 15	2×0	M 1×50	2 53	3 20	..	3 30	5 23	..	3×25	6 5	6×27	7 40
Titley arr.	1 18	1×19	2 3		CR	2×56	..	..	5×27	..	..		6 30	7 44
dep.	1×20	1 22	2 4			2 57	CS	3 34	3 35	5 33	..	CS	6×32	7 45
Forge Cross'ng dep.		1 27	..		..	..	..	..	5 38	..	..		..	..
Presteign arr.		1 38	..		..	3 40	..	..	5 49	..	..		..	..
Lyonshall dep.		..	..		..	..	3 39	3 45	..	..	..		..	..
Stop Board ,,		..	..	RR	..	..	..	..	..	..	S X		..	..
Almeley ,,		..	..	New Radnor	..	..	3 54	3 59	..	..	..		..	..
Eardisley arr.		..	..	to Dolyhir	..	..	4 5	..	..	..	..		..	..
Marston Halt dep.	1 26	2 10	..		..	3 3	..	..	..	..	..		6 38	7 52
Marston Sdg. ,,	—	..	..		CR	..	..	..	..	CR	..		..	..
Pembridge ,,	1 31	2 16	..		CS	3 9	..	..	..	3 42	4 0	6×25	6 43	7 57
Kingsland ,,	1 40	2 25	2 15		..	3 21	..	..	..	4 10	4 25	CS	6 52	8 6
Kington Junc. ,,	CS	OS	CS		CS	..	..	..	..	CS	CS	CS	..	CS
Leominster arr.	1 47	2 32	3 13		..	3 28	..	..	..	4 38	—	6 45	7 0	8 16

M Depart 1.45 p.m. Saturdays.
R To stop whether required for traffic purposes or not. **V** Runs on Kington and Presteign Cattle Sale days.
W To run Engine and Van only to Kingsland to cross 12.50 p.m. **RR** ex Hereford when latter runs.

6.0 p.m. Passenger Train ex Leominster. When from any special cause this Train is likely to be 20 minutes or more late from Leominster, that Station to communicate with Pembridge and Titley, and arrange for the 6.27 p.m. Passenger Train ex Kington to cross the 6.0 p.m. ex Leominster at Pembridge instead of at Titley. When this is done, the Pembridge Station Master must arrange for the Passengers in the 6.27 p.m. ex Kington to alight at Pembridge, after which the Empty Train will be set back into the Loop to allow the Train from Leominster to pass. As soon as the latter has left for Titley, the 6.27 p.m. ex Kington will be brought to the Platform at Pembridge, the passengers reloaded, and despatched to Leominster.

Traffic to and from Marston Siding (Pembridge). Traffic to or from this Siding will be dealt with by the 12.25 p.m. Goods Train ex New Radnor only when the 3.25 p.m. ex Kington runs at altered times, as on Kington Auction Sale days, and on Saturdays, otherwise work to be done by the 3.25 p.m. ex Kington. The Guard of either train must hand a memorandum each day to the Station Master at Pembridge shewing—

1st—What wagons he has put off at the Siding
2nd—What wagons he has picked up at the Siding

The numbers and contents to be shewn in each case and the labels of the inwards wagons to be attached to the memorandum.

3rd—If he has not attached or detached any wagons, a Nil memorandum must be given up, and he must shew on the Nil memorandum the total number of wagons there are in the Siding, Pembridge will advise Kington what wagons they may send to the Siding daily, and also consignees.

ENGINE ROUTES—NEW 0-4-2 TANK ENGINES, 48XX AND 58XX CLASSES.

Subject to the observance of Permanent Restrictions of Speed, it has been agreed to the above engines working over the following Branches:—

New Radnor, Presteign, Eardisley.

procedure for crossing passenger trains at Pembridge is described in a footnote on the page above of the Time Table.

Courtesy Michael Clemens

In mellow sunshine, a train, consisting of a pannier tank and a Worcester Division 'B Set', awaits departure from New Radnor. *Tony Harden collection*

which was attached a goods brake van. The latter was included in case it was desired to insert one or more non-continuously braked goods vehicles between the coach and the van, a step which converted the whole ensemble to a mixed train.

After the closure in 1951 to passenger traffic on the New Radnor extension and on the Presteigne branch, steam-worked auto-trains sometimes (for example in the summer of 1953) provided the surviving service between Leominster and Kington, as did they also on some local services on the S&HR main line between Leominster, Ludlow and Craven Arms, and on the branch to Tenbury Wells. In the public timetables from at least the summer of 1953 onwards, the Leominster and Kington service was stated to be 'Third Class Only', a description which would cover the use of auto-trains. It would appear that, although providing some other local services radiating from Leominster, the GWR diesel railcars were not used on the Kington lines.

The Second World War ...

On Monday, 1st July, 1940, all services on the Titley Junction to Eardisley branch were withdrawn. In the general scaling down of passenger train services during the Second World War, the service between Leominster and Kington was reduced, although a surprising feature was the provision of a late evening down train on Saturdays. An offsetting and important exception was the operation of ambulance and other special trains to convey wounded and traumatised service personnel to two major hospitals which were rapidly built in remote countryside at Hergest, some two miles south-west of Kington. These were the United States of America 107th and 122nd General Hospitals, both of which had a very large intake of casualties. The trains bringing them were long, sometimes consisting of ten or even twelve coaches, which needed to be gently moved, portion by portion, into the short platform at Kington so that the patients could be safely disembarked. To facilitate the transfer of the latter to local ambulances for the journey to Hergest, some of the railings along the Kington platform were removed. Another complication was that most of the hospital trains were air-braked (with the Westinghouse system), whereas GWR practice was to use the vacuum system. Consequently such air-braked trains were hauled by locomotives of other companies (often of the London and North Eastern Railway), coupled to a GWR locomotive which acted as pilot.

Only two passenger trains daily ran to and from New Radnor. The Presteigne branch also suffered a reduction to two return trains daily, one in the mid-morning and the other in the late afternoon. There were normally no Sunday trains anywhere on the system.

LEOMINSTER, KINGTON AND NEW RADNOR. (Week Days only.)

		a.m.	a.m.	a.m.	p.m.	p.m.	p.m.				a.m.	a.m.	a.m.		p.m.	p.m.	p.m.
Leominster	dep.	6 18	9 50		12 25	4 35	8 45		New Radnor	dep.			10 52			6 5	
Kingsland	"	6 29	9 59		12 50	4	8 54		Dolyhir	"			10 58			6 11	
Pembridge	"	6 38	10 7		1 2	5	9 2		Stanner Halt	"			11 2			6 15	
Marston Halt	"	6 44	10 12		1 9	5 11	9 8		Kington	arr.			11 10			6 21	
Titley	"	6 53	10 20	11 19	1 17	5 24	9 16		Kington	dep.	7 21	10 30	11 14	2 0	5 20	6 27	7 5
Kington {	arr.	6 57	10 24	11 22	1 24	5 28	6 21	9 18	Titley	"	7 26	10 33	11 18	2 3	5 24	6 32	7 9
{	dep.		10 28			5 33			Marston Halt	"	7 31		11 23	2 9		6 37	7 15
Stanner Halt	"		10 35			5 40			Pembridge	"	7 37		11 29	2 16		6 43	7 20
Dolyhir	"		10 39			5 44			Kingsland	"	7 46		11 38	2 26		6 52	7 28
New Radnor	arr.		10 45			5 50			Leominster	arr.	7 55		11 45	2 33		7 2	7 36

TITLEY AND PRESTEIGN. (Week Days only.)

		a.m.			p.m.					a.m.			p.m.	
Kington	dep.	10 30			5 20			Presteign	dep.	11 2			6 0	
Titley	dep.	10 34			5 28			Forge Crossing Halt	"	11 11			6 10	
Forge Crossing Halt	"	10 57			5 33			Titley	arr.	11 14			6 16	
Presteign	arr.	10 46			5 44			Kington	arr.	11 22			6 21	

KINGTON AND EARDISLEY. (Service Suspended.)

J—Through Service Dudley to Birmingham via Old Hill.
X—Third class only (limited accommodation).
Z—A Bus Service is operated between Halesowen and Old Hill by the Birmingham Motor Omnibus Co., Ltd. (" Midland Red ").
Q—Third class only.

The Second World War has taken its toll. This is the GWR timetable which took effect on 1st October, 1945. Only two trains now run through to New Radnor and the Presteigne branch has only two services each way daily. Service is 'suspended' over the Eardisley branch, which had in fact closed completely in July, 1940. Despite the cuts the late Saturday evening train from Leominster to Kington has survived.

Table 176 — LEOMINSTER, TITLEY, KINGTON, and NEW RADNOR

Miles		Week Days only					Miles		Week Days only			
		a.m a.m		p.m p.m p.m					a.m a.m		p.m	p.m p.m
—	Leominster........ dep	6 18 9 50	..	1235 4 55 9 5	..		—	New Radnor........ dep	.. 1050	..	..	6 5 ..
4¼	Kingsland.............	6 29 9 59	..	1250 5 4 9 14	..		2¾	Dolyhir.............	.. 1055	..	..	6 10 ..
8	Pembridge...........	6 38 10 7	..	1 2 5 12 9 22	..		3¾	Stanner Halt........	.. 1059	..	..	6 14 ..
10	Marston Halt.........	6 44 1012	..	1 9 5 17 9 28	..		6¾	Kington (below).. { arr	.. 11 5	..	..	6 20 ..
12	Titley...............	6 52 1020	..	1 17 5 24 9 35	..			dep	7 20 11 7	..	2 10	6 25 7 5
13½	Kington (below).. { arr	6 57 1024	..	1 24 5 28 9 39	..		8¼	Titley..............	7 25 1112	..	2 15	6 32 7 9
	dep	.. 1028	..	.. 5 33	..		10¼	Marston Halt........	7 30 1118	..	2 20	6 37 7 14
16½	Stanner Halt.........	.. 1035	..	.. 5 40	..		12¼	Pembridge..........	7 37 1124	..	2 25	6 43 7 20
17¾	Dolyhir.............	.. 1039	..	.. 5 44	..		16	Kingsland...........	7 46 1133	..	2 35	6 52 7 29
20¼	New Radnor........ arr	.. 1045	..	.. 5 50	..		20¼	Leominster........ arr	7 55 1140	..	2 42	7 27 36

Table 177 — KINGTON, TITLEY, and PRESTEIGN

Miles		Week Days only					Miles		Week Days only			
		a.m		p.m	p.m				a.m		p.m	p.m
—	Kington........... dep	1028	..	1 10	5 20	..	—	Presteign......... dep	1055	..	1 55	6 0 ..
1¾	Titley........ { arr	1031	..	1 15	5 25	..	4	Forge Crossing Halt....	11 4	Sats. only	2 5	6 10 ..
	dep	1032	..	1 20	5 28	..	5¼	Titley........ { arr	11 8		2 11	6 16 ..
3½	Forge Crossing Halt...	1034	..	1 25	5 32	..		dep	1114		2 15	6 17 ..
7¼	Presteign......... arr	1044	..	1 35	5 44	..	7½	Kington........ arr	1117	..	2 22	6 22 ..

By the autumn of the first year of Nationalisation, a third service over the Presteigne branch has been re-introduced, but on Saturdays only. The New Radnor extension still has only two trains each way daily, and the late Saturday evening train between Leominster and Kington now runs earlier. This is the Western Region timetable operative from 27th September, 1948, and, with very minor changes, it remained current until early in 1951, when the national coal shortage led to the suspension of all services upon the Kington lines.

The Western Region timetable for 18th June to 23rd September, 1951, is almost identical to the September, 1948, one above but erroneously lists trains between Kington and New Radnor and trains on the Presteigne branch. Those two sections had lost their passenger services during the fuel shortage in February of that year and never regained them. Presumably the timetable was compiled and printed before the final decision had been taken not to restore them.

Table 176 — LEOMINSTER, TITLEY, and KINGTON

Miles		Week Days only							Miles		Week Days only			
		a.m a.m		p.m	E	S	S				a.m a.m		p.m	p.m
		3 3		3							3 3		3	3
—	Leominster........ dep	6 18 9 50	..	1235 4 55	..	5 35	8 25	..	—	Kington........... dep	7 20 11 7	..	1 50	7 5 ..
4¼	Kingsland............	6 29 9 59	..	1250 5 4	..	5 43	8 34	..	1¾	Titley.............	7 25 1112	..	1 55 7	9 ..
8	Pembridge...........	6 38 10 7	..	1 2 5 12	..	5 51	8 41	..	3½	Marston Halt........	7 30 1118	..	2 07	14 ..
10	Marston Halt.........	6 44 1012	..	1 9 5 17	..	5 57	8 47	..	5½	Pembridge..........	7 37 1124	..	2 57	20 ..
12	Titley..............	6 52 1020	..	1 17 5 24	..	6 5	8 52	..	9¼	Kingsland...........	7 46 1133	..	2 15 7	29 ..
13½	Kington........... arr	6 57 1024	..	1 24 5 29	..	6 9	8 57	..	13½	Leominster........ arr	7 55 1140	..	2 23 7	36 ..

E Except Saturdays.   S Saturdays only.   3 Third class only.

The timetable for 8th June to 20th September, 1953, shows only the section between Leominster and Kington, over which passenger services had recommenced on 2nd April, 1951. The '3' at the head of each column probably means that the services were provided by an auto-train (which had no first class accommodation). With minor changes, this timetable continued until closure.

Table 176 — LEOMINSTER, TITLEY, and KINGTON (Third Class only)

Miles		Week Days only						Miles		Week Days only			
		a.m a.m		p.m p.m		p.m S				a.m a.m		p.m	p.m
—	Leominster........ dep	6 18 9 50	..	1235 4 55	..	8 25	..	—	Kington........... dep	7 20 11 7	..	1 50	7 5 ..
4¼	Kingsland............	6 29 9 59	..	1250 5 4	..	8 34	..	1¾	Titley..............	7 25 1112	..	1 55	7 9 ..
8	Pembridge...........	6 38 10 7	..	1 2 5 12	..	8 41	..	3½	Marston Halt........	7 30 1118	..	2 07	14 ..
10	Marston Halt.........	6 44 1012	..	1 9 5 17	..	8 47	..	5½	Pembridge..........	7 37 1124	..	2 57	20 ..
12	Titley..............	6 52 1020	..	1 17 5 24	..	8 52	..	9¼	Kingsland...........	7 46 1133	..	2 15	7 29 ..
13½	Kington........... arr	6 57 1024	..	1 24 5 29	..	8 57	..	13½	Leominster........ arr	7 55 1140	..	2 21	7 36 ..

S Saturdays only.

During the currency of this timetable for 20th September, 1954 to 12th June, 1955, the passenger service between Leominster and Kington was withdrawn, on 7th February, 1955.

... and its aftermath

Hostilities ended in 1945, but the Kington lines never fully recovered. The last GWR timetable of all, operative from 6th October, 1947, shows five return services between Leominster and Kington, two of which continued to, and returned from, New Radnor. By September, 1948, the wartime two return services over the Presteigne branch were increased, on Saturdays only, by a third, mid-day, service, but, whereas after the First World War the Eardisley line had been reopened (in 1922) this time it remained closed.

Table 176	LEOMINSTER, TITLEY, and KINGTON—(Third class only)		
Miles		Week Days only	
—	Leominster .. .. dep	SERVICE SUSPENDED	
4¼	Kingsland		
8	Pembridge		
10	Marston Halt............		
12	Titley		
13¼	Kington .... arr		

Miles		Week Days only
—	Kington .. .. .. dep	SERVICE SUSPENDED
1½	Titley	
3¾	Marston Halt	
5¼	Pembridge	
9¼	Kingsland	
13¼	Leominster .... arr	

After the withdrawal of the passenger service between Leominster and Kington, the Western Region continued for some years to include Table 176, but only to state that the service was suspended.

The Worcester connection

Reference has already been made to the working of through trains between Worcester and Kington and New Radnor. The extent of this integration varied over the years, but here is a typical example.

In the summer of 1938, a train left Worcester (Shrub Hill) at 8.05 am, and made an unhurried journey via Bromyard to Leominster, arriving there at 9.26. Here it paused before setting off again at 9.52, and then called at all stations to New Radnor, reached at 10.45. At this terminus there was a surprisingly rapid turn-round of only five minutes, and the train was scheduled to start its return journey at 10.50. At 11.41 it was due at Leominster, where it connected with the southbound 11.50 main line train, and where again there was an interval before, at 12.20 pm, it resumed its journey to Bromyard and to Worcester (Shrub Hill), where it finally arrived at 1.40.

Curiously, the time allowed for station work at New Radnor was quite limited. The morning through train from Worcester was scheduled to arrive at New Radnor at 10.45 am and to depart at 10.50.

During this brief period it was necessary to uncouple the engine, and to run it forward to the buffer stops, where it was reversed to enter the quite long run-round loop. Then the ground frame at the eastern end of the station had to be unlocked with the train staff, and the engine placed on the running line, from where it would set back onto the coaches and be attached. Finally there would be a brake test and the repositioning of head and tail lamps. This rapidity seems to be hardly congruent with the generally measured proceeding of trains on the line.

An interesting instance of co-ordination arose in the post-war period. At 6.25 pm on weekdays in the summer of 1951, a diesel railcar departed from Kidderminster for Bewdley and the Wyre Forest line. When it reached Woofferton Junction at 7.24 it ran not into the normally used bay platform situated on the west side of the station but into the down main line (towards Hereford) platform. Two minutes later it left, and, after calling at the intermediate station of Berrington and Eye at 7.33, arrived at Leominster at 7.40. Here it had been preceded by the arrival at 7.36 by the 7.5 all stations from Kington train. Another 6.25 pm departure, this time from Shrewsbury, had been an all stations (except Condover and Wistanstow Halt) train, which followed the diesel railcar from Woofferton and arrived at Leominster at 7.51 before running non-stop to Hereford. Finally, and 4 minutes later, the railcar departed at 7.55 for Bromyard and Worcester (Shrub Hill), where, after calling at all intermediate stations, it arrived at 9.11. This combination of arrivals at and departures from Leominster enabled passengers from the Kington and Shrewsbury lines to reach Bromyard and Worcester the same evening, and also allowed passengers from the Kington line stations to travel promptly to Hereford. Alas, the former facility came to an end in the following year. The operation of through trains to and from Worcester necessarily came to an end when all passenger services over the line between Leominster and Bromyard were withdrawn on Monday, 15th September, 1952. There being no trains on Sundays, the last train over this section ran on Saturday, 13th September, 1952.

The distance between Worcester and Leominster via Bromyard was 8½ miles shorter than the route via Hereford, and this difference was reflected in the fares. For example, the *ABC Railway Guide* for December, 1951, lets us know that the 1st class single fare from Paddington to Leominster via Bromyard (148 miles) was 48s. 1d., and via Hereford (156½ miles) was 49s. 1d. The corresponding 3rd class fares were 28s. 11d. and 29s. 5d. (so one could enjoy an extra 8½ miles of 3rd class travel for 6d.!).

OPERATION OF THE LINES

This extract from the December, 1951, issue of the *ABC Railway Guide* indicates that the Worcester – Bromyard – Leominster route was regarded as normal for travel between London (Paddington) and Kington. Alas, this route would cease to be available on and from 15 September, 1952, when the passenger service between Bromyard and Leominster was withdrawn.

Author's collection

KINGTON (Hereford)
Map Sq. 17. Pop. 1,890. Clos. day Wed.
From **Paddington** via Bromyard and Leominster 161¾ miles.
1st cl.—Single 52/8, Mth. Ret. 63/6.
3rd cl.—Single 31/9, Mth. Ret. 42/4.

Padd.	Kington	Kington	Padd.
a.m.		a.m.	
1 0∥	10 24	7 20	2 15
5 30	1 24	11 7r	5 5
11 45r	5 29	p.m.	
p.m.		1 50r	9 5
4 45r	9 44	7 5∥	4 25
—	—	—	—

No Sunday Trains.

∥ Via Hereford and Leominster.
e Not Sat.   s Sat. only.
r Refresh. Car.

But not the only route, as demonstrated by this table showing alternatives via Hereford and Shrewsbury.

Author's collection

LEOMINSTER (Hereford)
Map Sq. 17. Pop. 6,289. Clos. day Thur.
REFRESHMENT ROOMS.
From **Paddington** via Worcester and Bromyard 148 miles.
1st cl.—Single 48/1, Mth. Ret. 57/11.
3rd cl.—Single 23/11, Mth. Ret. 38/7.

Padd.	Leom.	Leom.	Padd.
a.m.		a.m.	
5 30	11 41	7 0r	11 30
11 45r	3 47	8 45	2 15
p.m.		p.m.	
4 45r	9 5	12 20r	5 5
—	—	4 20†r	9 5
—	—	—	—

No Sunday Trains.

† Connection at Worcester, Foregate Street
e Not Sat.   s Sat. only.
r Refresh. Car.

Another Route
From **Paddington** via Hereford 156½ miles.
1st cl.—Single 49/1, Mth. Ret. 59/3.
3rd cl.—Single 29/5, Mth. Ret. 39/6.

Padd.	Leom.	Leom.	Padd.
a.m.		a.m.	
1 0	9 38	5 8r	10 45
5 30	12 8	9 16r	3 5
9 45r	3 14	11 42r	5 5
11 45r	4 46	p.m.	
p.m.		2 28r	9 5
2 15	8 17	7 51	4 25
—	—	—	—

Sunday Trains.

a.m.		a.m.	
10 10r	8 18	5 0r	2 50
—	—	p.m.	
—	—	3 14r	9 25

e Not Sat.   s Sat. only.
r Refresh. Car.

Another Route
From **Paddington** 191 miles or **Euston** 201 miles via Shrewsbury.
1st cl.—Single 51/11, Mth. Ret. 62/9.
3rd cl.—Single 31/3, Mth. Ret. 41/10.

Padd.	Eust.		Leom.
a.m.	a.m.		
12 5	—		8 0
9 10	—	r	2 28
11 10	—	r	5 26
p.m.			
2 10	—	r	7 51
4 10	—	r	9 48
—	9 25	s	5 0
—	10 45	e	5 8
—	—		—

Sunday Trains.

a.m.	a.m.		p.m.
12 5	12 30		3 14
11 10	10 50	r	6 34
—	p.m.		
—	10 50		5 8
—	—		

From Leominster.

Leom.	Eust.		Padd.
a.m.			
7 57	g	—	2 15
7 57	r	—	2 35
9 38	r	4 12	5 5
p.m.			
12 8	r	—	5 35
3 14	r	—	8 40
4 46	gr	—	10 25
4 46	kr	—	11 35
8 17		3 29	5 5

Sunday Trains.

a.m.			
10 12	r	6 20	—
10 12		—	7 50
p.m.			
8 18		3 37	—

e Not Sat.   r Refresh. Car.
g Fri. & Sat.   s Sat. only.
k Not Fr. or Sat.
Bus facilities. From Hereford, Bus Stn., approx. hourly, 40 min. journey.

Goods traffic

The goods conveyed by the Kington lines were many and varied. Coal inwards was foundational, for it was needed for domestic use in areas which mainly had no gas or electricity supply, and for industry, particularly in Kington, which was home not only to the notable foundry of the Meredith family but also to a range of other manufacturers; and it was needed too for the lime works and kilns situated along the New Radnor extension. Finished goods were also carried to all stations, along with the necessities of agriculture, including machines and fertilisers.

Goods traffic outwards included corn and cereals and fruit and vegetables, and the products, such as iron and woollen goods, of the various industries located in Kington. Much livestock, ranging from chicks to cattle, was carried and in the early autumn vast numbers of sheep were exported from the hill farming areas just beyond the western end of the network. The staple traffic from the New Radnor extension consisted of limestone – to be used for buildings and for roads – and of lime with its many practical applications. The dominant user of the New Radnor extension was undoubtedly the Old Radnor Trading Company.

Stanner station (from 28th July, 1941, halt) on the extension to New Radnor, looking west. The station building is similar to that at the K&ER station at Almeley on the Eardisley line. The goods yard is largely the preserve of the Old Radnor Trading Company.

John Alsop collection

The Old Radnor Trading Company Limited

This became the abbreviated name of the Old Radnor Lime, Roadstone, and General Trading Company Limited, which was formed in 1875, the year in which the extension of the K&ER to New Radnor was completed. The company's first chairman was Charles Chambers, the contractor who had, after many changes of plans and builders, intervened to complete, most expeditiously, the K&ER line from Eardisley to Titley, and who had between 1873 and 1875 efficiently constructed the K&ER's 'detached' length of railway between Kington and New Radnor.

The hilltop village of Old Radnor was, like 'Clunton and Clunbury, Clungunford and Clun', one of 'the quietest places under the sun',* although the military fortifications and works in its vicinity spoke of a different and turbulent past. Upon the shoulders, and at the foot, of the eminence upon which the village stood there were, however, quarries rich in limestone and in other minerals, some of which were similar to the valuable 'dhu' stone found further north on Clee Hill, near Ludlow. The far-sighted Charles Chambers saw that the aggregates which were here available could be used nationally to make new roads and to upgrade existing roads, many of which were of indifferent construction, alignment, and upkeep. He leased the quarry areas from their owner, the Reverend Sir Gilbert Frankland Lewis, who was the third baronet of Harpton Court, and upon whose land the western end of the New Radnor line was built and indeed upon which New Radnor station itself stood.

The quarrying and despatch of roadstone were in addition to the production of lime in the kilns, which continued to thrive. The outputs from these activities were carried in private owner wagons bearing the name of the trading company. In the early years of the twentieth century, there were probably as many as two hundred of these wagons, painted in a bluish grey colour with bold white lettering, and, laden with stone, they were sent to many different parts of the country. Rather than let them be returned empty, the ever expansionist Mr Chambers arranged for many of them to be loaded with coal directly bought from collieries, and he then set up depots in many Welsh Border towns and villages to sell the fuel. Deprived of any continuation into the fastnesses of the Cambrian Mountains, the New Radnor extension thus had a new raison d'être: a staple traffic of minerals in both directions.

The wooden-bodied wagons of the Old Radnor Trading Company had a hard life, being constantly loaded with heavy minerals such as limestone and coal, and in most years as many as fifty of the fleet required repair and renovation.

---

* Quoted from A. E. Housman, *A Shropshire Lad*.

Marston siding

Marston siding was connected to the running line by means of a turnout facing down trains. It could therefore be served only by up goods trains travelling from Kington. The goods guard had to complete a memorandum stating how many vehicles, if any, he had set down and picked up at the siding, and hand this to the station master at Pembridge, who would inform Kington of the state of affairs. It could then be calculated how many further wagons could be accommodated at the siding when the next up goods train was being marshalled.

Goods traffic ends

Goods traffic ceased at New Radnor on and from Monday, 31st December, 1951, but continued for several years on the remaining parts of the Kington lines. Goods trains ran as far as Dolyhir until they were withdrawn on Monday, 9th June, 1958; and thereafter to Kington and Presteigne until late September, 1964, although by late in 1963 they were running only on Tuesdays and Thursdays, and (usually to Kington only) on Saturdays. Goods facilities at Titley had been withdrawn on Monday, 6th July, 1959. One of the last (and probably more remunerative) duties was the conveyance of pipes for a new gas network at Presteigne. The goods train service was officially withdrawn on Monday, 28th September, 1964, and the last recorded freight train ran on Thursday, 24th September, hauled by 0-4-2 tank locomotive No. 1420.

Motive Power

In the early years of the Leominster and Kington Railway trains were worked by locomotives belonging to the contractors, Brassey and Field, who, until the end of June, 1862, were also responsible for operating the train service. These engines were, possibly, named *Bateman*, in honour of the chief proponent of the line and chairman of the L&KR; and *Brassey*, the principal contractor. The West Midland Railway (WMR) took over operation of the line on and from 1st July, 1862, and, it would seem, allocated to the L&KR two 2-4-0 Crewe pattern well tank locomotives built by Jones and Son of Liverpool. It would also seem likely that these engines continued to work over the line for several years after the amalgamation in 1863 of the WMR with the GWR, who numbered the

A mixed train stands at the platform of Presteigne, hauled by an 0-4-2 saddle tank locomotive.
John Alsop collection

engines 229 and 230. Thereafter the GWR supplied the motive power, at first in the form of 0-6-0 saddle tank locomotives, and later by tank engines of the 2-4-0 and 0-4-2 wheel arrangements. The latter included members of the celebrated Armstrong '517' class, designed and built at Wolverhampton. During the 1930s these faithful, but by then outmoded, locomotives were, in the main, gradually supplanted by Collett 0-4-2 tank engines of the 4800 and 5800 classes (first introduced in 1932), which then became largely responsible for working the lines until their closure. One older engine which did survive was 0-4-2 tank engine No. 3574, built in August, 1895, as a member of William Dean's numerically small '3571' class. This engine continued to work on the Kington lines alongside the more modern 4800 and 5800 tank engines, and was still active during the early part of the Second World War. It was then relegated to shunting and steam raising in the works at Worcester, but towards the end of, and after, the war No. 3574 had a further spell of working passenger trains between Worcester and Leominster and on the Kington lines until it was finally withdrawn on Saturday, 31st December, 1949.

The lines to Eardisley and to Presteigne were from their outsets also worked by GWR engines. The engines concerned were again of the 0-6-0 saddle tank type, and later came 0-4-2 tank engines, some of them of the versatile '517' class. Tank engines of the 2-4-0 wheel arrangement were also used. In later years, the Collett 0-4-2 tank engines were the mainstay of the motive power. They were clearly suited to the nature of traffic over the two lines.

Although tender engines of the 'Dean Goods' ('2301') and of the '2251' series were also used from time to time on the Kington lines (for example, during the week during which the water tank at Kington underwent its annual cleaning), tank engines were generally preferred, since there were no turntables on any of the lines concerned. Additionally, tank engines were ideally suited to the lengths of journey and train weights usual on these lines. After Nationalisation, however, former LMSR Ivatt 2-6-0 ('mogul') engines (which had tender half cabs and which were popular with engine crews on the HH&BR and Mid-Wales lines) were occasionally to be seen on goods trains.

Although many local passenger services in the Worcester motive power district (including some which originated or terminated at Leominster and travelled via Bromyard) were provided by diesel railcars of GWR origin, it would seem that such vehicles were never, either regularly or even at all, used on the Kington lines.

Engine Sheds
Leominster

The original engine shed at Leominster was situated at the south (Hereford) end of the station. Opened in 1853, at the time of the

Locomotive No. 1420 standing outside the engine shed at Leominster. *Oakwood Press*

completion of the Shrewsbury and Hereford Railway, it was a substantial brick building (approximately 70 feet x 35 feet), having large, round headed, windows. It accommodated two roads, one of which continued at the rear of the shed to reach a coaling stage and turntable. On 1st January, 1901, the complement of this original shed consisted of 0-6-0 saddle tank No. 2035, a recently-built member of the Dean '2021' class, and 0-4-2 tanks Nos. 542 and 1422, both of which were members of the Armstrong '517' class.

In 1901 this engine shed was demolished in the course of the alteration and enlargement of Leominster station, and was replaced by a brick-built two road shed of (then) modern design at the north end of the station, together with a 45 feet turntable. The new shed had convenient access to the three platforms used by trains running over the lines to Bromyard and Worcester, and to Kington and New Radnor. To the east of the shed lay a coaling platform and crane; and a sand drier was provided next to the shed eastern wall.

In 1921 the newer shed was host to 0-4-2 tanks Nos. 827, 1432 and 1487, all again of the Armstrong '517' class; 0-6-0 tank No. 1765, of the Dean '1854/1701' class; and 0-6-0 tanks Nos. 2109 and 2146, both of the Dean '2021' class. (Much later, some of the '1400' series numbers of by then withdrawn engines of the '517' class were used for the new Collett 0-4-2 tank locomotives.)

In 1947, just prior to Nationalisation, the inhabitants of the by now long established 'new' shed were 0-6-0 pannier tank locomotive No. 2714, and Collett 0-4-2 tank locomotives Nos. 1455 and 1460 (both auto-fitted), and Nos. 5807 and 5817 (both non auto-fitted). These Collett engines were used on passenger trains on the local services on the 'North and West' main line as well as on the Kington lines. Subsequently, engines of the '7400' series of pannier tank engines were installed at Leominster to work goods trains on the surviving Kington lines. They were in turn succeeded (from early in 1962) by locomotives of the '1400' class for handling goods traffic. In these later years, 0-4-2 tank locomotives Nos. 1420 and 1447 worked many goods trains on the branches before the service was finally discontinued in September, 1964. The last recorded train ran on Thursday, 24th September, 1964, and was hauled by No. 1420.

Leominster was within the main Worcester Division and accordingly lay within the sphere of Worcester motive power depot (coded 85A by the Western Region of British Railways). For most practical purposes, however, Leominster shed was a sub-shed of Hereford, which itself reported to Worcester and was coded 85C, but was largely autonomous. In February, 1960, Hereford shed was transferred to the control of Ebbw

Junction (Newport)(then 86A), and was re-coded 86C in the following year. At the same time, Leominster was nominally transferred to Shrewsbury (89A), but in practice continued to be an outstation of Hereford. In April, 1962, the shed at Leominster was closed, and thereafter two locomotives for Leominster duties were sent 'light engine' daily from Hereford. These duties included working the goods trains on the Kington lines, and shunting the still-extensive goods yards at Leominster. The two engines usually ran coupled together between Hereford and Leominster.

Kington

A brick-built, slate roofed, engine shed, measuring approximately 60 feet x 20 feet, was built in 1875, the year in which the 'new' Kington station was opened and in which services to Stanner, Dolyhir and New Radnor began. The shed was situated to the west of the station and on the north side of the line; and a small coaling stage was provided. Water was supplied from a large, elevated, tank situated to the north of Kington station, and was then made available from cranes located at the west end of the (new) station down platform; at the east end of the up platform there; and also in the goods yard (the former terminus of the L&KR). A very tall up home signal which was sited between the Sunset road overbridge and the platforms of Kington (new) station was later replaced by a new up home signal opposite the shed so as to protect any engine movements which might be taking place.

In 1902 the shed accommodated two class '2021' saddle tank locomotives, Nos. 2027 and 2035 (the latter had previously been kept at Leominster). In 1921, two other members of the same class, Nos. 2151 and 2153, were housed in Kington shed. On 31st December, 1947, the eve of Nationalisation, the locomotive allocation consisted of two Collett 0-4-2 tank engines, Nos. 5808 and 5814 (both non auto-fitted). Three engine crews were stationed at Kington shed. When passenger services over the Kington lines were suspended after the end of traffic on Saturday, 5th February, 1951, the shed was closed, and was never reopened.

There were no engine sheds at New Radnor, at Presteigne or at Eardisley.

Signalling
Methods

Initially all of the Kington lines were operated by single line train staff, a method which remained in use throughout the history of the Eardisley and Presteigne branches and on the New Radnor extension. Between Kington Junction and Kington there were three staff sections, namely Kington Junction and Pembridge; Pembridge and Titley; and Titley and Kington. In addition, Kingsland was a block post, but not a staff station.

By 1873 staff and ticket working had begun to be added to the sections between Leominster (Kington Junction) and Kington, and, although Kingsland was not a staff station, its presence as a block post enabled line capacity between Kington Junction and Pembridge to be increased when the staff and ticket system was in operation. Under the Regulation of Railways Act, 1889, the GWR was obliged to install the absolute block system on all passenger-carrying lines, and on the Kington line this requirement was met in 1891. The busy single line section between Titley Junction and Kington was upgraded to electric train staff (ETS) working in 1898. In 1906 this ETS system was installed

A striking view of the elevated signal box situated on the long island platform at Leominster. Note the LMSR coaches standing at the short island platform.

Author's collection

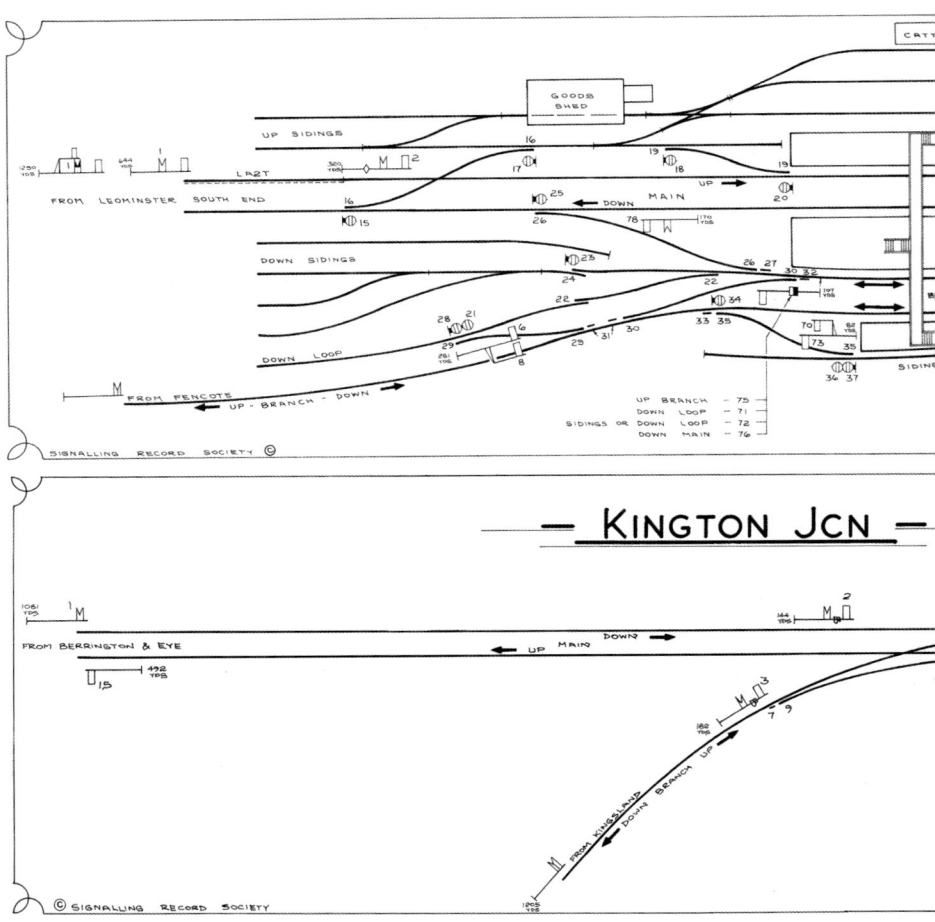

on the rest of the main line between Kington Junction and Titley Junction. At some point between 1943 and 1952, the ETS between Pembridge and Titley was replaced by a key token.

After regular passenger trains had ceased to run (on and from Monday, 7th February, 1955), the surviving parts of the Kington lines were operated in two sections: Kington Junction to a point just beyond Pembridge; and from there to Kington and Presteigne. This arrangement enabled one goods train to attend to Leominster and Pembridge traffic, while another was busy on the rest of the line. The boundary between the sections was indicated by a board placed at 7 miles and 69 chains, 20 chains beyond Pembridge station. These two sections were united on

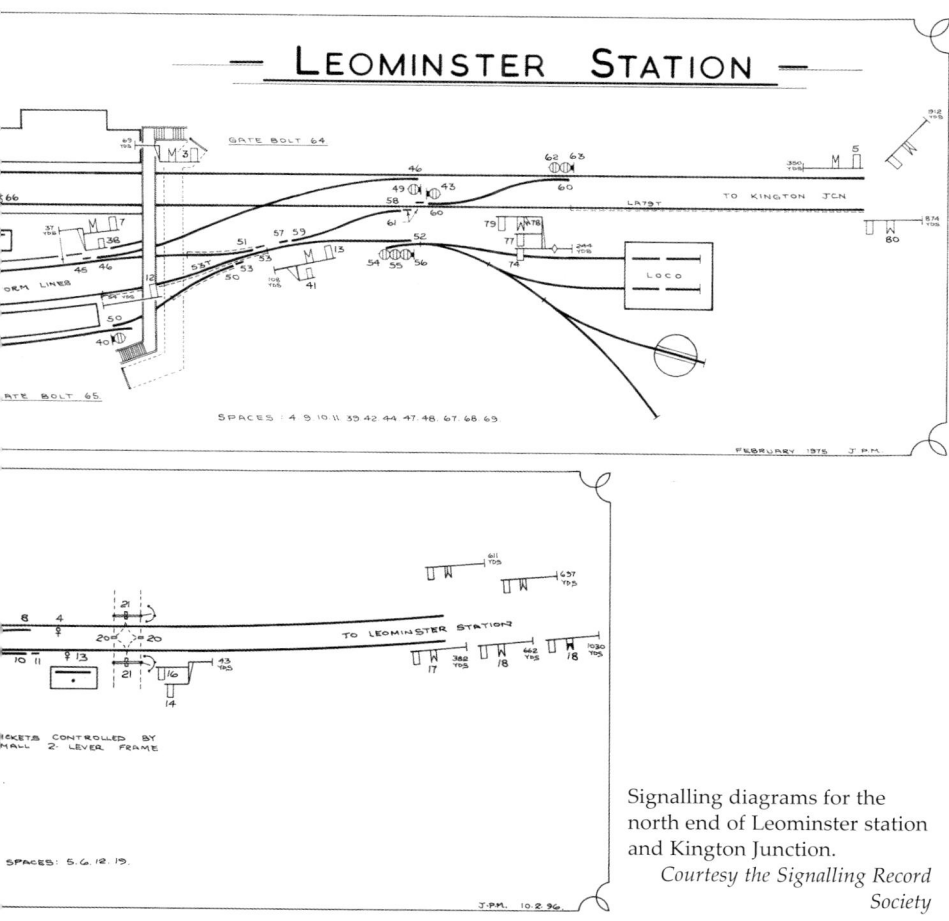

Signalling diagrams for the north end of Leominster station and Kington Junction.
Courtesy the Signalling Record Society

and from Monday, 6th August, 1962, and from then the whole of the surviving Kington lines system was operated upon the one engine in steam principle. After leaving Kington Junction on the outward journey, the guard placed three detonators on the track, and the fireman removed them upon the return of the train from Kington.

Kington Junction

At Kington Junction, 34 chains north of Leominster station, the signal box, situated on the west side of the main line, controlled a level crossing (over the present road A49) as well as the junction itself, where the branch took the usual form of double track converging to form a single line. The box contained 19 levers, including 4 spares. In addition, there was a separate small frame having 2 levers for locking the pedestrian wicket gates.

Kingsland

Here a signal box was provided at the western (Kington) end of the single platform from 1874. Alterations to the station track layout and signalling in 1902 were accompanied by the replacement of this box by a new one (of GWR type 6 design) situated at the eastern end of the platform. It was adjacent to the level crossing, which was protected by the down home signal and by the up starting signal. The box had 15 levers, including 5 spares; and, as at Kington Junction, there was a separate 2 lever frame controlling the wicket gates.

At the western end of the station layout was a siding loop (not used for crossing trains). Later the sidings were further extended to serve a sawmill, but these changes did not affect the signalling arrangements. The points at the far end of the loop were operated from a small ground frame, which was released by lever 10 in the signal box (see the diagram), or, at certain times, by Annett's key attached to the train staff.

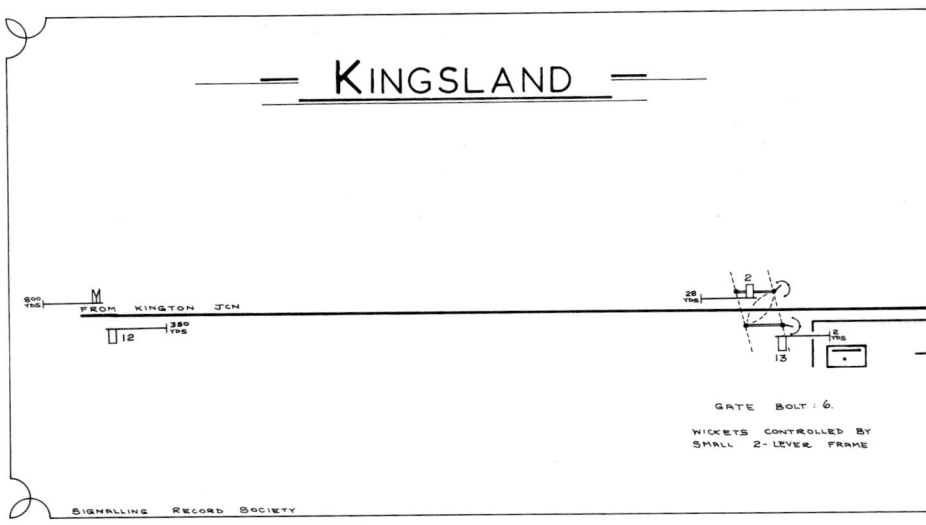

Courtesy the Signalling Record Society

Pembridge

The history of the layout and of the signalling arrangements at Pembridge is a little complicated. From 1880 there was a signal box (having 10 levers) at the Kington (western) end of the station's platform alongside the single running line. This box controlled admission to a loop, at the western end of which a ground frame controlled the points where the two lines of the loop converged.

From 1902 the layout at Pembridge was controlled by a new signal box (of GWR type 7b, with 33 levers). This box was located alongside the up (eastbound) side of the loop, which was now fully signalled, and which enabled trains to cross or to overtake one another. Its position enabled it to control both ends of the loop. Incidentally, the timber upperwork of this signal box had been designed and made for installation at the Dolphin signal box (situated between Langley and Slough on the main line between Paddington and Reading), but had been reallocated to Pembridge.

In the mid 1920s the GWR conducted a study of many of its secondary and branch lines, with a view to making economies in their running costs. In consequence, it was decided to simplify the arrangements at Pembridge, and in particular to convert the crossing loop to a siding loop. The Dolphin signal box alongside the up side of the loop was abolished in 1927, and was replaced by a smaller, redundant, box, which

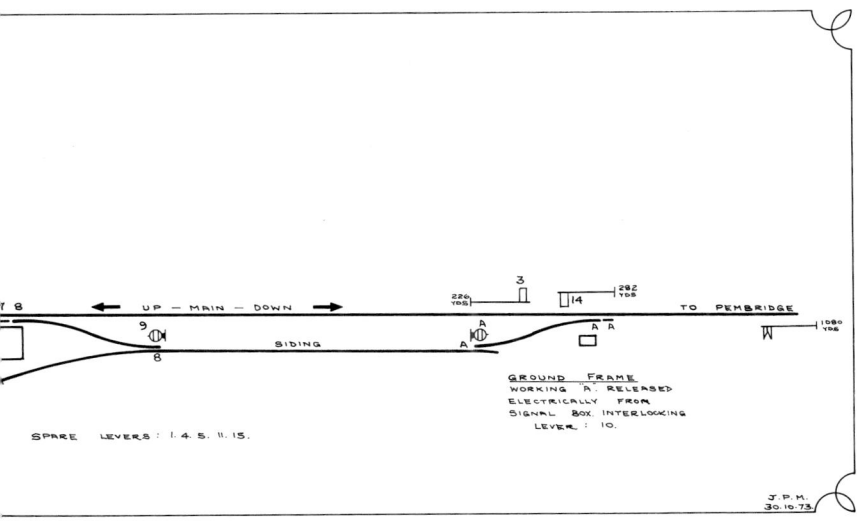

was transferred from Cilcewydd (also spelt Kilkewydd), situated between Welshpool and Forden on the Cambrian main line, and which was now installed immediately to the west of the level crossing at the east end of the station. (It was this crossing which had given rise to the difficulties when the line was opened (*see pages 15 – 16*).) The 'new' box had 12 levers, two of which were spare. From this time onward, the former up loop line was normally to be used both by up and by down trains, and the former down side of the loop became a loop siding. The status of the two lines was clearly indicated by the configuration of the bracketed down starting signals at the west end of the station (see the photograph).

The points at the far western end of the loop were henceforward controlled from a new and adjacent ground frame (Pembridge West Ground Frame), which could be unlocked by a key forming part of the Pembridge and Titley electric train staff. The accompanying diagram shows (only) the points and signals controlled by the signal box which was adjacent to the level crossing. In fact, 'Siding No. 1' on the diagram continued westwards to connect with what was now the main running line, the points being controlled by the ground frame already mentioned (and that is why the convergence is not included in the signal box diagram: the ground frame was independent). Later still, in 1958 (three years after the final withdrawal of regular passenger train services), the up-main-down side of the loop was removed, and the former down side of the loop ('Siding No. 1') became the running line (see the photograph).

Pembridge was not normally regarded as a crossing place for passenger trains, since there were no passenger platforms adjacent to the loop. At one time, however, there was an interesting partial exception. The GWR service (working) timetable for 1936 lets us know that the 6.00 pm passenger train from Leominster to Kington was booked to call at Titley from 6.29 to 6.32. Here it was due to cross a passenger train which had left New Radnor at 6.05 pm and was scheduled to call at Titley from 6.30 to 6.32. If, however, the departure of the 6.00 from Leominster was delayed by more than 20 minutes (for example, because of late running main line connecting services), the train from New Radnor was permitted to advance to Pembridge, so as to minimise delay to passengers bound for Leominster and beyond. The station master at Pembridge then had to ask the ex-New Radnor train passengers to alight and to remain on the Pembridge platform, while the by now empty train set back into the loop. The train from Leominster could then call at the platform, and, after restarting, pass the empty train. The latter could now run forward from the loop to the platform, and the displaced passengers could resume their seats. This procedure may not have been entirely well received on wintry evenings.

OPERATION OF THE LINES

The goods yard at Pembridge. The 'Dolphin' signal box (1902-1927) is visible behind the main running line.
Michael Hale/Great Western Trust

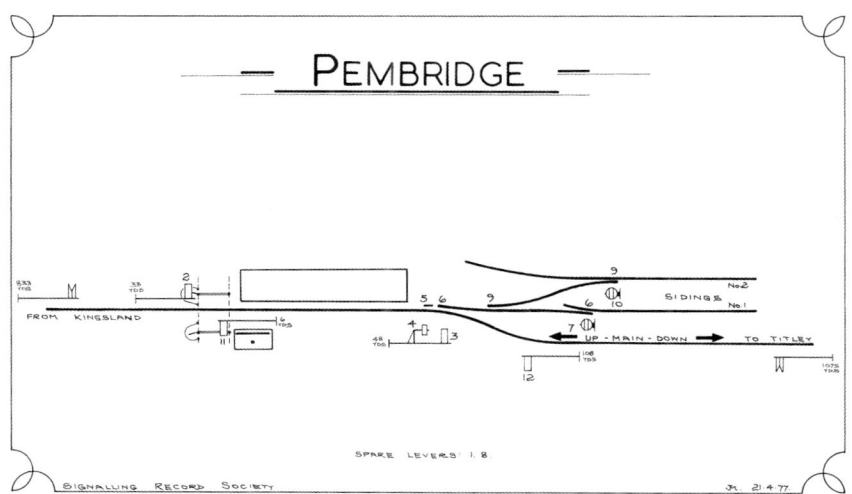

Courtesy the Signalling Record Society

Titley

A new, and large, signal box at Titley came into operation in 1902. It contained 37 levers, as many as 11 of which were spares. The starting signal on the up (eastbound) platform had a single arm, below which was an indicator having plates inscribed 'PRS'TN' (lever 33); 'LM'STR' (lever 34); and 'ERDS'LY' (lever 35), informing the train crew and station staff about the route (Presteigne, Leominster, or Eardisley respectively) to which the signal arm itself referred when it was lowered. The nameplate on the front of the box said simply 'Titley Signal Box', whereas the name-boards on the station read 'Titley Junction for Presteign and Eardisley'. A similar state of affairs arose at Woofferton, on the North and West main line, and the junction for the secondary line which ran to Tenbury Wells and Bewdley. On the signal box name-plate and in the public and service (working) timetables, the station was known simply as Woofferton, whereas the name-boards on the platforms expansively read 'Woofferton Junction: Change for Tenbury Wells and Bewdley Branch'.

Titley box was closed in August, 1958, by when it had become superfluous following the simplification of the line and the installation of a hand-worked point at the junction with the Presteigne branch (*see page 40*).

Some years ago Titley Junction station and a length of trackbed leading towards Kington were purchased by a private buyer.

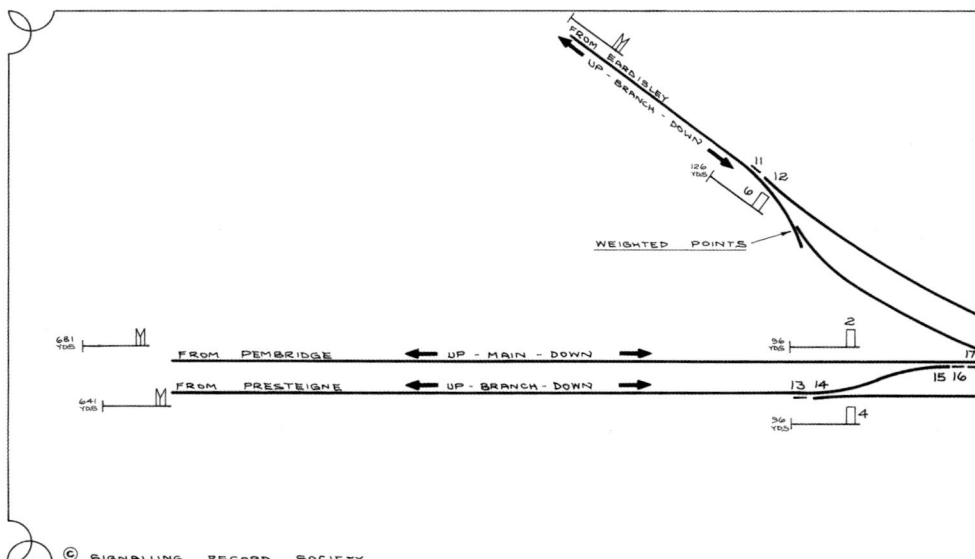

Courtesy the Signalling Record Society

Restoration work is in hand, and various items of rolling stock and other material of railway interest have been gradually acquired. The site is, however, essentially private and is not open to the public except on occasional open days.

Titley Junction, looking east. The line to Eardisley diverges to the right immediately beyond the platforms. The left of the two parallel lines in the middle distance is for Presteigne and the right is for Leominster. Note the route indicator on the up line starting signal, an unusual feature at a country junction. Note also the pronounced quoins and the small sheltering canopy on the down side building. *John Alsop collection*

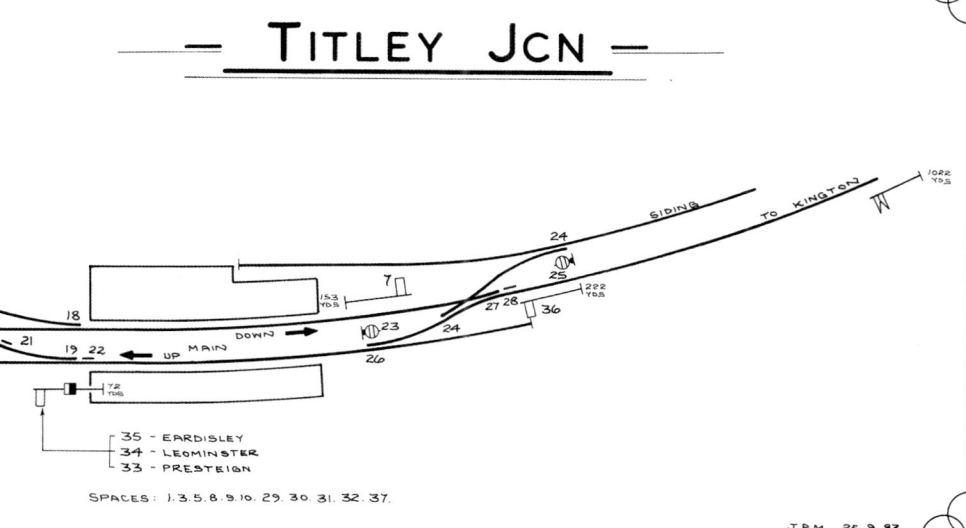

Kington and the New Radnor extension

When the layout at Kington was remodelled between 1902 and 1905, a new signal box was provided on the north side of the main running line, and the visibility over the layout was very good. There were 23 levers, of which one was spare. The up home signal governing access from the New Radnor extension originally stood on the east side of Sunset Bridge, but was moved further west (to a position 323 yards from the signal box), so that movements to and from the engine shed could be made within station limits and hence would not occupy and so block the New Radnor section (see the diagram).

There were no signals at Stanner. Admission to the sidings there was controlled by a ground frame released by the wooden train staff. Dolyhir was not a crossing station or block post, and the distant signals placed at the approaches to the two level crossings were worked independently by the crossing keepers. These signals were of course lowered only when the gates of the crossings had been secured against road traffic. A platform-mounted ground frame, released by the train staff, controlled the sidings at Dolyhir.

At the approach to New Radnor there was a fixed distant signal to remind drivers of the terminus ahead, and the signal had a lamp-in/lamp-out repeater in the station office.

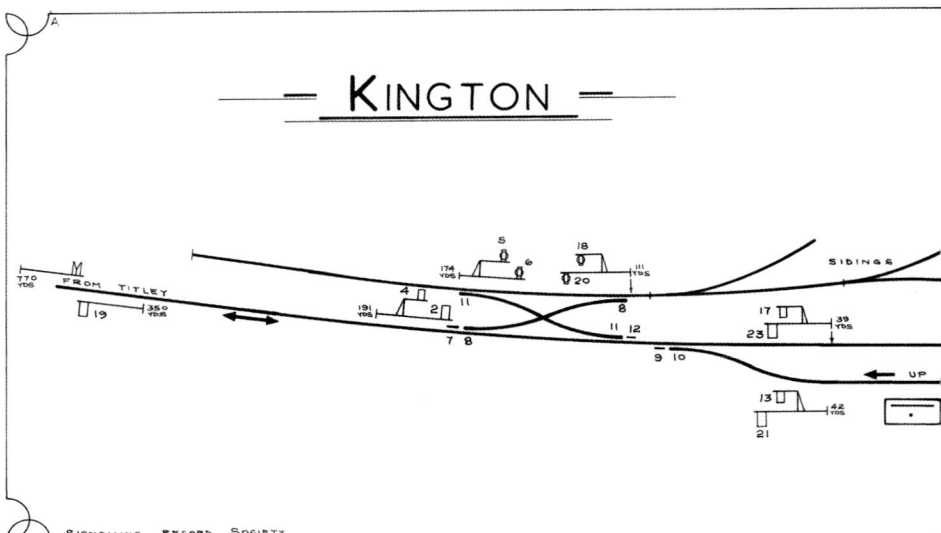

Courtesy the Signalling Record Society

The line to Eardisley

Trains had begun to run on Monday, 3rd August, 1874, over the Kington and Eardisley line between Titley Junction and Eardisley Junction, and the junction between the K&ER and the HH&BR was controlled by Eardisley Junction signal box, situated 5 chains east of Eardisley station. A new box at the junction was in use by November, 1875, the year after which the Midland Railway, which was already operating the HH&BR, had taken a lease of the line. This box at Eardisley Junction was in turn replaced by a new one of typically Midland design on 18th June, 1893, one year after the electric train tablet system had been installed along this section of the HH&BR. The box was modified when the K&ER was closed on 1st January, 1917, and was further altered when that line was fully re-opened on 11th December, 1922. More changes followed when services over the K&ER were finally withdrawn on 1st July, 1940. A short section of the southern end of the K&ER was retained so as to provide access to a fuel depot and to store spare passenger coaches. This connection was eventually removed on 21st August, 1955. Eardisley Junction signal box itself was closed when all remaining services over the HH&BR ended on 28th September, 1964.

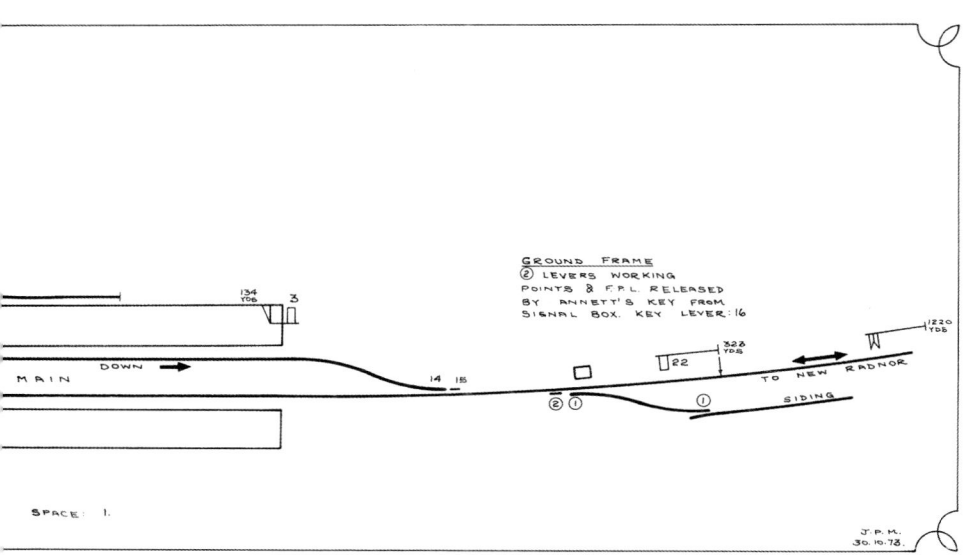

The Presteigne Branch

Admission to the Presteigne branch was controlled by the signals at Titley (already described). The level crossing at the Forge was under the control of a gatekeeper, who operated two distant signals, one in either direction. At one time Presteigne station itself had a signal box, and until at least the beginning of the twentieth century there were some signals, including a distant signal at the approach to the station, a home signal to control entry to the station itself, and a starting signal to allow trains to commence their journeys to Titley. It would seem, however, that, after acquiring the L&KR outright, the GWR came to consider these signals unnecessary upon a line which was worked strictly upon the one engine in steam principle; and that in consequence the signals were abolished, and that thereafter the points for the loop and sidings were worked by ground frames. These frames were released by a key attached to the wooden train staff, which throughout the history of the line was the sole authorisation for all train movements. At the northernmost end of the layout the entry point for the run-round loop was worked by a simple hand-lever.

Signal box hours of opening

The signal box at Kington Junction was open continuously (this was natural, as it was located on the 'North and West' main line). The boxes on the Kington line opened sequentially: for example, in 1936 and in 1945 that at Kingsland opened at 6.00 a.m., that at Pembridge at 6.10, and those at Titley Junction and at Kington at 6.30. They closed in the evenings after the passage of the last train. None of the boxes along the line was provided with a switch, and hence they all needed to be staffed while the line was in use. The line was normally closed to traffic on Sundays.

Speed Restrictions

A speed limit of 15 mph applied to all trains joining or leaving the branch at Kington Junction, and trains entering, traversing and leaving the loops at all stations on the Kington Lines system were required not to exceed 10mph. In addition, a restriction to 15 mph was imposed upon certain curves upon the New Radnor extension and the Eardisley and Presteigne branches.

Chapter Three

A Journey Over the Lines in the 1930s

Leominster to Kington

A substantial station was provided at Leominster when the Shrewsbury and Hereford Railway (S&HR) between Ludlow and Hereford was opened in 1853. Two long platforms were constructed. On the west side of the station, the up (towards Shrewsbury) platform, later numbered No. 1, included the main building. Consisting of two storeys, it had low hipped roofs, and its architecture was typical of that of other S&HR stations. Adjacent to this building was a pump house, surmounted by a large water tank. The lengthy down (towards Hereford) platform was an island. The inner face (platform 2) was alongside the down main line, while the outer face (platform 3) served a loop, frequently used by the Kington line trains. This island afforded cross platform interchange for passengers proceeding from the down direction to the trains for Kington, and vice versa.

In 1884, and in anticipation of the opening of the line to Bromyard and Worcester, a further island platform was added on the east side of the

Leominster station looking north from the long island platform, with the main station buildings on the left and the short Bromyard platform on the right. *John Alsop collection*

layout. This new platform (with faces 4 and 5) was much shorter than the first island, but was extremely useful: it could accommodate Kington as well as Bromyard trains when platform 3 was already in use or otherwise not available. 1884 was the year in which, on 1st March, trains began to run to Steens Bridge, although it would not be until 1st September, 1897, that trains started to run all the way to Bromyard and to Worcester.

Leominster station was much enlarged, and was resignalled, at the beginning of the twentieth century, although the main buildings situated on the west side of the station remained after these changes. Alterations included the re-ordering of the yards to the south of the station, and the replacement of the S&HR engine shed by a new shed at the north end of the layout.

The most striking new feature of Leominster station was the elevated signal box, which stood on the long island platform (faces 2 and 3). This signal box was of London and North Western Railway (LNWR) design, and dated from 1901. The box was supported not only by a single row of uprights on the platform, but also by horizontal bracing cross girders resting on pillars standing on the island platform with faces 4 and 5. This highly unusual arrangement in some measure resembled that at Atherstone on the LNWR Trent Valley line, where the raised signal box stood in the middle of the station and between the down and up fast lines. The Atherstone box also dated from the early part of the twentieth century. The boxes at both locations provided exceptionally good visibility over the stations, even though they were assailed by billows of smoke and steam.

Trains for the Kington and New Radnor line usually left from either platform 3 or 4 at Leominster station. Platform 5 was normally the preserve of trains departing for their long journey to Bromyard and Worcester, but could also be used by Kington line trains. In general, however, platform 3 was the most favoured, as it was long enough to accommodate two trains at the same time (one for Bromyard and Worcester, and one for the Kington line), and, as noted above, it also afforded cross platform interchange with platform 2.

Upon leaving Leominster station, the Kington line trains had to cross the down main line and then joined and followed the up (towards Ludlow and Shrewsbury) main line, until they reached Kington Junction, 34 chains from Leominster station. (A comparable situation obtained at Woofferton (6¼ miles north of Leominster), where a bay platform was constructed on the west side of the main line. To reach and leave this bay, Tenbury Wells and Bewdley line trains had to cross both up and down main lines.)

A JOURNEY OVER THE LINES IN THE 1930s

In Leominster station: two typical auto-trains stand at platform 5.
Michael Hale/Great Western Trust

A local train stands at platform 3 at Leominster. The elaborate bracing girders help to support the signal box, here partly obscured by smoke and steam.
Tony Harden collection

At Kington Junction the branch line trains diverged, and turned westwards into the broad plain of the River Lugg to run alongside one of the river's tributaries, the Pinsley Brook. This brook rises at the Lady Pool in the Shobdon Marshes and resembles a chalk stream in the south of England. A short distance from the junction the railway crossed, on the level (at the 'Marsh Crossing'), the Leominster to Richards Castle road (the present B4361), and, further along, the line crossed, again on the level, the road (the present B4360) leading from the small settlement of Cobnash to Kingsland village (this was known as the 'Waterloo Crossing'). Another level crossing, this time over the Hereford to Wigmore road (the present A4110), immediately preceded Kingsland station, 3 miles and 72 chains from Kington Junction, and the railhead for the charming 'black-and-white' village of Eardisland, situated on the River Arrow and just over two miles south-west of the station.

Kingsland station consisted of a single platform, on the north side of the line, and was provided with large two storey brick station buildings, which, with their gables and steeply-pitched roofs and stone lintels, presented an imposing sight. The range included the station

Kingsland station, looking towards Leominster. Its substantial buildings belie the fact that it was a simple wayside station. The signal box, of GWR pattern 6, dates from 1902, and replaced an earlier (c.1874) box situated at the west end of the station layout.

John Alsop collection.

master's house. At the eastern end of the platform, and close to the level crossing, stood the signal box. To the north of the box was a dwelling house, originally provided for a crossing gatekeeper (when the signal box was at the western end of the station), and latterly available for a porter/signalman. The neo-Tudor architectural style of the house was similar to that of the main station buildings. Again, the main material was brick, and the facings were of dressed stone.

Beyond the western end of the platform a siding in the form of a loop, serving a goods shed, was situated on the north side of the line, but Kingsland was not a crossing station. Admission to the furthermost (western) end of the loop siding was controlled by a ground frame (*see page 68*). There were some simple cattle pens, and a short spur from the east end of the loop led to an end-loading dock which was situated just to the west of the passenger platform and which was useful for handling agricultural machinery. To the north of the goods area, and also reached from the loop, were sidings serving a sawmill, which became an important source of traffic for the line. Between 1933 and 1944 the sawmill was operated by the firm of W. H. Aston, and at other times by Kingsland Sawmills Limited.

The railway continued its generally westward course, and, at 4 miles and 44 chains from Kington Junction, crossed on the level another minor road, which ran from Kingsland to Ledicot and Shobdon. This intersection was named Brook Bridge Level Crossing after the Pinsley Brook, which at this point flowed just to the north of the railway. The line then turned south-westwards to cross the Shobdon Marshes, passing en route Ox House station, which took the form of a private platform provided for Shobdon Court. The Court lay some two miles to the north and was reached by a footpath from the railway. On the north side of the line lay Shobdon airfield. There is no certain date for the closure of Ox House station: it probably fell out of use after the partial demolition of Shobdon Court, but it may later have been unofficially used to provide access to Shobdon airfield (which, incidentally, still exists).

Pembridge, the next station, was also immediately preceded by a level crossing. It was the unauthorised construction of this crossing which caused difficulties when the line was inspected. The station, at 7 miles and 49 chains from Kington Junction, was generally similar to that at Kingsland, but this time the platform and station buildings were on the south side of the line. The signal box was situated to the west of the level crossing and opposite the passenger platform. The signalling history of Pembridge has been described above.

The line continued into a goods loop, while the running line itself turned briefly to the right and then ran parallel with the loop before rejoining it at the west end of the layout. (For the operation of this loop in exceptional circumstances, *see above, page 70*.) Beyond the passenger station, and on the south side, stood a commodious goods shed, adorned with decorative Gothic arcades which were surmounted by dressed keystones. It was almost square in plan, and could accommodate several wagons. A little way further to the west a set of cattle pens was provided, and further to the south a travelling crane assisted the trans-shipment of goods from rail to road, and vice versa. The crane was of six tons capacity.

After rejoining the siding loop at the west end of the Pembridge station area, the running line now pursued a generally westward course all the way to Kington. Shortly before Marston Halt, facing points led to a short siding ('Marston Siding', 9 miles and 34 chains from Kington Junction) situated on the south side of the line. In this vicinity the authorised, but never constructed, line between the K&ER and Presteigne would have intersected the L&KR.

The level crossing visible in the middle distance was made in contravention of the Leominster and Kington Railway Act, 1854, which stipulated that a bridge should be made at this point. The level crossing was subsequently legitimised by the Leominster and Kington Railway Amendment Act, 1859. The signal box was transplanted from Cilcewydd (near Welshpool) and succeeded the earlier 'Dolphin' signal box located alongside the loop line behind the camera. The bracket signal in the foreground makes it clear that this loop line was the main line for down as well as for up trains.

Tony Harden collection

A JOURNEY OVER THE LINES IN THE 1930s

Marston Halt built in 1929.

J. Peden/Stations UK
Middleton Press from album 'Ludlow to Hereford'

A minor road, leading from Staunton-on-Arrow to Marston village, crossed the line on the level, just before Marston Halt (9 miles and 40 chains from Kington Junction), which was situated on the south side of the line. Opened on Friday, 26th April, 1929, the halt was located on or near the site of the original Marston Road (or Marston Lane) station, and it consisted of a full height timber built platform on which stood an arc roofed shelter made of corrugated-iron. Oil lamps were provided at each end of the platform. The halt was thus quite similar to that opened at Forge Crossing earlier in the same year.

Approximately one mile beyond Marston another railway came in from the north and ran parallel with the main line as far as Titley Junction. This additional line was the branch to and from Presteigne. The resultant appearance of the two lines was one of double track, but the reality was that they were two independent lines. Shortly before Titley Junction what appeared to be a trailing crossover between the two tracks enabled trains from Presteigne to reach the down platform at Titley Junction station, 11 miles and 48 chains from Kington Junction. Immediately east of the station a double junction brought in the line from Eardisley; and at this junction a single slip enabled trains to move from the up platform onto the line leading to Leominster.

Titley Junction looking east. *John Alsop collection*

Situated in quite isolated countryside, and about 1½ miles south of the small village of Titley, the junction station was extensive. There were two side platforms, and the main buildings lay on the down (Kington bound) side. Once again, the station building had two storeys, and was constructed of brick and stone, with tall chimneys. The corners of the building were remarkable for their heavily accented stone quoins. A small canopy, reminiscent of those at Newnham Bridge and at Neen Sollars on the Tenbury and Bewdley line, was attached to this building and offered some, although limited, protection from the weather. The opposite (up, eastbound) platform was, however, devoid of shelter.

The signal box of 1902 was impressive. Situated on the up side and close to the double junction for the branch to Eardisley, the box was unusually long, and contained 37 levers (including 11 spares) as well as the instruments required for trains travelling in four different directions: in clockwise order, these were towards Pembridge and Leominster; Eardisley; Kington and New Radnor; and Presteigne.

At the west end of the layout, and on the south side of the line, was a goods siding with a head-shunt located in the direction of Kington. A weighbridge, with a brick and timber office, was provided, and there was a small store for goods, but the main rôles of the station were those of an interchange, junction, and passing place. Titley Junction did not have its own water supply, and fresh water was delivered (in churns) by train. In later years (from 1947) a former milk tank wagon was stationed in the siding behind the down platform in order to store water.

The two running tracks of the loop singled, and the railway now ran close to the River Arrow for some of the way to Kington, where it originally terminated in the eastern part of the town in the locality known as 'Sunset'. The railway by now ran somewhat north of the River Arrow itself (which flows to the south of Kington), and on the approach to Kington crossed a stream, which was known variously as the Back Brook or as the Langdale Brook, a tributary of the River Arrow. The through line leading to the passenger station and so to the New Radnor extension ran to the north of, and parallel with, the original L&KR line which terminated at the first (1857) passenger station. This original line then formed a lengthy head-shunt, and between it and the new running line was situated a scissors crossover which greatly facilitated shunting operations. The layout provided considerable flexibility in working ,and it was possible for shunting to take place independently in the goods yard while the main running line was in use by trains proceeding to and from the new passenger station.

The 'new' (1875) station at Kington, looking east. The stream flowing under the bridge in the foreground is the Back Brook (or Langdale Brook), a tributary of the River Arrow. The very tall signal post is that of the original home signal for trains coming from the New Radnor extension. It was later replaced by a signal sited further to the west, so as to bring the engine shed within station limits. *John Alsop collection*

At the first (1857) Kington passenger station, two platforms were provided and alongside that on the north side of the line was a two storey station building, generally similar to, and with the same pronounced quoins as, that at Titley. The two platform lines formed the longest sidings in the goods yard after they ceased to be used for passenger trains.

We have seen that the position of this first station at Kington had made it impossible to continue the line further, and the westward extension of the standard gauge railway along the general course of the Kington Railway (the tramway) had necessitated the realignment of the main line, and the construction of a new passenger station just to the north of the original terminus. The latter, however, remained in use as a goods station until the complete closure of the line. This sequence of events is remarkably similar to that which occurred at Witney in Oxfordshire, where the original terminus in the town was superseded by a new station built slightly to the north when the East Gloucestershire Railway to Fairford was constructed. Similarly, at Tenbury the original and temporary (1861) terminus of the branch line from Woofferton was replaced by a new through station to the north when the line from Bewdley arrived in 1864.

In April, 1954, an auto-train from Leominster arrives at the 'new' (1875) station at Kington, in the care of Collett 0-4-2 tank locomotive 1455, which frequently worked on the line. Note the unusually positioned water crane on the passenger platform. The prominent, bracketed, home signal controls admission to the New Radnor extension, which was then still open as far as Dolyhir.   *Dr A. J. G. Dickens/collection C. G. Maggs*

The 'new' (1875) passenger station at Kington (13 miles and 28 chains from Kington Junction) was situated a short distance to the north of the L&KR terminus, and indeed the goods shed of the latter was close to the main building on the down side of the K&ER station, which took the form of a passing loop with two side platforms. As the original L&KR station and sidings continued to be used as the goods depot for Kington, the new K&ER station was used mainly for passenger and for parcels traffic. The building was smaller and simpler than those at the other L&KR stations, but, in common with them, had a steeply pitched roof. A small waiting room on the up platform had an arched entrance. Water cranes were provided towards the west end of the down platform and at the east end of the up platform. They were supplied from a large free-standing water tower which stood behind the up platform. Kington station was illuminated by gas lamps, supplied from the town's gas works, which had been founded as early as 1830, and then rebuilt in 1873. Other stations on the Kington lines were lit by oil.

The signal box stood at the eastern end of the up platform, and thus had an excellent view of the approaches to the station. The down line through the passenger station was not truly reversible, as incoming trains from the New Radnor extension could not use it. The down platform could, however, be used to start up trains, as a starting signal was provided beyond the eastern end of the platform, and this arrangement simplified operations at the station, since it was possible for terminating down trains to commence their return journeys without first transferring to the up platform. This facility was also for the convenience of passengers, who did not need to leave the down platform and to cross the line to the up platform, except in the case of the trains arriving from New Radnor. To gain access to the up platform it was necessary to use an unsurfaced (and hence potentially hazardous) crossing at the west end of the station. No passenger footbridge was provided at Kington, or indeed at any of the other stations on the Kington lines.

On to New Radnor

Immediately to the west of the K&ER station at Kington, the line re-crossed the Back Brook (or Langdale Brook), and then passed under a bridge, known as the Sunset Bridge, which carried the road leading from Kington to Titley, Rodd and Presteigne (the present B4355). Next, there was situated on the north side of the line the Kington locomotive shed. This single road shed could accommodate two small tank locomotives, and was the signing on point for the three engine crews who were responsible for many of the workings on the Kington lines. To the east of the shed itself was situated a small coaling stage. Water was available from the water cranes (already mentioned) located at the passenger station. The main line in this vicinity was sharply curved, and, to assist visibility for enginemen, the home signal controlling admission to Kington station was sited on their right hand (south) side of the line. This signal was also positioned so that trains arriving from New Radnor and Dolyhir could be held outside the station area while locomotives moved to and from the shed.

The railway now continued westwards, and broadly parallel with the course of the Kington Railway (i.e. the tramway) to a level crossing known as 'The Floodgates', and then it closely followed the Back Brook and the trunk road (the present A44) leading to New Radnor, Rhayader, and ultimately Aberystwyth. The railway passed under this road, and from now on ran at varying distances to the south of this important thoroughfare.

The railway crossed the border between England and Wales and so entered Radnorshire. About ¾ mile beyond this boundary, the train entered Stanner station, at 16 miles and 18 chains from Kington Junction. Situated on the north side of the line, the platform and station buildings and goods yard occupied a space between the railway and the trunk road. The simple stone station building was adjoined by a (separate) brick built lamp room. The platform also accommodated a small corrugated lock-up shed for goods traffic. Behind the platform, and bordering the main road were two sidings. One was constructed when the railway was first built, and was chiefly used for quarry traffic. The second siding was added in September, 1914, primarily for the benefit of (and funded by) the Old Radnor Lime, Roadstone and General Trading Company. The sidings also served the coal depot operated by the local firm of Walter Morgan. They were reached by a turnout which faced down trains at the east end of the station, and which was controlled by a ground frame released by the train staff. The frame was housed in a small hut, and comprised 3 levers: 1 controlled a facing point lock and 2 worked the points to the sidings. There was no separate goods shed: parcels and small items of high value could be safely stored in the lock-up shed on the platform itself. A loading gauge stood near the turnout from the running line. Stanner was reclassified as a halt on and from Monday, 28th July, 1941, and from then on was no longer staffed. The nameboard, however, remained unchanged.

The plain station buildings at Stanner, at Dolyhir and at New Radnor were quite dissimilar to the lavish brick edifices of the L&KR. It was, on the other hand, unsurprising that these stations resembled that provided on the K&ER at Almeley, between Lyonshall and Eardisley, since the New Radnor extension was also built and owned by the K&ER. The stations on this extension were essentially adaptations of a design which had originally been prepared for Dolyhir, but which was subsequently modified in the interests of economy. The outcome was the provision at each station of a plain, single storey building, rectangular in plan, made of stone, and having a simple pitched slate roof. A modest decorative feature was added in the form of ornamental barge boards.

On leaving Stanner, the line passed the tiny settlement of Burlingjobb, the terminus of the Kington Railway (the tramway which had, in conjunction with the Hay Railway, provided the through route to the Watton Wharf at Brecon). To the north lay the steeply-inclined Old Radnor Hill, upon which stood the ancient village and castle of Old Radnor. The railway now reached Dolyhir (17 miles and 32 chains from Kington Junction), lying in the midst of the quarries and works which had been the chief raison d'être for the K&ER extension to New Radnor, and indeed for the K&ER itself.

Stanner station, looking east towards Kington. The brick building next to the main building is a lamp room, and the windowed corrugated-iron shed behind the name board is for parcels. The loading gauge can also be seen. The small shed to the right of the track in the mid-distance houses the ground frame controlling access to the sidings behind the platform.

Lens of Sutton Association

Dolyhir station, looking east, and set amid the Radnorshire hills. The plain stone building is typical of those on the New Radnor extension. The nearer, brick, building is a lamp hut.
John Alsop collection

On parade at Dolyhir. The shunters proudly hold their poles like churchwardens' staffs, and locomotive 1552, with triple headlamps, has been polished for the occasion.
John Alsop collection

Dolyhir ('Long Meadow') station lay between two level crossings ('East' and 'West'), each of which was provided with distant signals controlled from ground frames in the care of a crossing keeper who lived in a purpose built cottage. (The red 'targets' on the crossing gates constituted the 'stop' signals to which, in each direction, the distant signals referred.) Each ground frame contained 3 levers: 1 was a gate lock, and each of the other 2 was connected with one of the distant signals.

The station resembled that at Stanner, in being provided with a single platform on the north side of the running line, and with a sturdy stone building. This was a simplified version of the original design, the modification consisting of the omission of one of the originally planned two waiting rooms. Again, there was a brick built lamp room, and also a corrugated-iron lock-up shed for goods. A small ground frame of 5 levers, housed in a hut at the western end of the platform, and unlocked by means of the train staff, controlled the points in the vicinity of the station itself (and was quite separate from the ground frames which controlled the distant signals at the two level crossings). These points controlled access to gated sidings leading to Strinds Lime Works (located at the east end of the station layout), and to the extensive North Kilns and South Kilns (situated on either side of the line at the west end of the layout). These North and South Kilns belonged to, and were worked by, the Old Radnor Trading Company.

Upon leaving this unwonted and almost astonishing scene of industry in deeply rural Radnorshire, the line curved briefly left, and then turned right to take up a generally north-westerly course almost as far as the terminus. Most of the route from Kington had been on rising gradients, but the final section into New Radnor was level. To the south, and tending to dominate the small station, was a hill called 'The Smatcher'.

The destiny of the railway station was strangely congruent with that of the village whose name it bore, and short of which it stood by just over a quarter of a mile. 'New' Radnor – which was in fact hundreds of years old, having been founded in the eleventh century – was intended to be a walled town to succeed the ancient settlement of Old Radnor, some three miles to the east, and it began to be laid out as a carefully planned town, with a gridiron pattern of streets. But the plan foundered, and was never taken to fulfilment. New Radnor became the village which it remains to this day, set in surroundings of great natural beauty.

Similarly, the railway station never attained its envisaged purpose. As built, New Radnor station (19 miles and 66 chains from Kington Junction) was evidently intended to be a crossing station on a line to Rhayader or Builth and beyond, as is evinced by the fact that the platform

Another general view of New Radnor station. The steep hill on the left is 'The Smatcher'.
Lens of Sutton Association

line diverged from the straight line which was envisaged as the up line of a passing loop. But no platform was ever built alongside this up line, which in practice served the purpose of a run-round loop for engines which had brought their trains to rest at this remote railway outpost.

The platform stood on the south side of the line, and upon it stood a main building similar to those found at Stanner and at Dolyhir (and so to that at Almeley). Minor distinguishing features were that the roof was slightly more steeply inclined, and thus a little higher, than those of the buildings at its fellow stations; and the barge boards were slightly more elaborate. Again, there was a brick-built lamp room (these rooms were needed to tend and to supply with oil the lanterns ranged along the platforms).

To the south of the passenger platform lay a small goods yard. The alignment of the two sidings was slightly altered from time to time over the course of the station's history, but a neat stone-built goods shed and a cattle dock were retained as built. A loading gauge was provided, and was once changed to a then more modern design.

The loop points at the further (western) end of the station were worked by a simple, weighted, hand-lever, but at the nearer (eastern) end there was a ground frame, housed in a hut on the northern side of the line, and released by the train staff. The frame contained 4 levers, of which two controlled facing point locks, another the loop points, and the other the access to the sidings. A fixed distant signal acted as a landmark for trains approaching the terminus.

Beyond the buffer stops lay the Radnorshire hills, receding into the distance, and at once both beckoning and forbidding.

From Titley Junction to Presteigne

Eastwards from Titley Junction the branch line to Presteigne ran parallel with the main line of the L&KR for a distance of about one mile before curving to the north. For most of their existence, there was no junction between the two lines at their divergence, but, after the Kington lines network had been reduced to a goods only service, a connection was laid (in 1958) where the lines met, and then only a single line remained all the way to Titley and Kington. The new hand-worked points were operated by the train crew.

At one mile and 50 chains from Titley Junction stood Forge Crossing Halt. This halt, which was opened on Saturday, 9th March, 1929, was of a simple character: on the east side of the line there was a short, timber edged, platform, illuminated by two oil lamps and provided with a small, arc-roofed, corrugated-iron hut. Immediately to the north of the halt were crossing gates protecting a lane leading eastwards for about

Forge Crossing Halt, looking towards Presteigne. The halt was opened on 9th March, 1929, but the crossing gates date from much earlier. The windowed hut beyond the crossing contains a ground frame controlling a gate lock, and distant signals in both directions.

Lens of Sutton Association

two miles towards Staunton-on-Arrow, which was (in a sense) also served by Pembridge station, which was again about two miles from that village. To the north of the crossing and on the east side of the line a small house was provided for the crossing keeper.

About one mile north of Forge Crossing the line veered to take up a generally north-westwards course to Presteigne. It passed to the east of the small settlement of Rodd, and then crossed, at Wegnall, the Hindwell Brook, which was a continuation of the Summergill Brook (a stream which actually rose near New Radnor), and which was a tributary of the River Lugg. At Wegnall the railway crossed the county boundary between Herefordshire (England) and Radnorshire (Wales).

Presteigne station

The originally planned site for the station at Presteigne was altered so as to bring the railway closer to the town centre. The layout also opened the possibility, never fulfilled, of extending the railway to Knighton or to Llangunllo, where a junction might have been effected with the Central Wales line. Consequently, the station at Presteigne (5 miles and 57 chains from Titley Junction) was – like that at New Radnor – laid out not as a conventional terminus, but rather as a through station. At Presteigne the

The overgrown platform and loading dock and the removal of the station canopy impart a forlorn appearance to Presteigne station, here seen from the buffer stops.
Tony Harden collection

passenger platform was located on the east side of the running line, and further to the east was a goods yard, with a goods shed, cattle dock, weighbridge, and loading gauge. A run round loop was provided alongside the platform line, and terminated at a side and end loading dock.

The passenger station building was of a design influentially developed by William Clarke, examples of whose work were to be seen in many places in the West Midlands and in the South West. William Clarke was an accomplished civil engineer, and was reportedly a brother in law of David Wylie, engineer to the S&HR, to the L&KR, and to other railways. When, sadly, David Wylie died in 1863 at the early age of 53, William Clarke succeeded him in his role as engineer to the Tenbury and Bewdley Railway.

What became known as Clarke's 'standard' design for station buildings was, essentially, for a single storey building, rectangular in plan, constructed of warm red brick and Bath stone, and having distinctive, accented, stone quoins at the corners and at the window surrounds. Such buildings had a simple, pitched roof (often of Broseley red tiles), which was surmounted by tall, ornate and heavily-built chimneys, again with stone quoins. There was a canopy extending the width of the platform, and inclined slightly downwards to the main building, so that rainwater could flow to a valley. This canopy was supported by several large brackets attached to the platform side main wall of the building, and hence there was no need for supporting posts on the platform itself. At Presteigne, the canopy was removed in about the year 1950, much to the detriment of the appearance of the building, which thereafter presented a stark, almost desolate, sight. Near the north end of the platform stood a lamp hut made of corrugated-iron; and at the south end had stood a small signal box.

From Titley Junction to Eardisley

The Kington and Eardisley Railway began its independent course by diverging from the Leominster and Kington Railway at the eastern end of Titley Junction station. As was usual in instances of this kind, a double junction led from the main line which ran through the station, and then the two lines of the branch converged to form the single line which continued to Eardisley. This first section of the branch abounded in sharp curves and steep gradients. It reached a summit, the second highest on the line, and then dropped steeply at 1 in 47 before entering a switchback section leading to Lyonshall station, one mile and 44 chains from Titley.

The buildings and facilities at Lyonshall station, one mile and 44 chains from Titley, were perhaps surprisingly elaborate. The passenger platform was situated upon an embankment, and at its southern end it spanned a road (the modern A480). Here there was located a substantial stone station building of two storeys, one at ground level, where passengers could gain entry, and from where stairs led to the first floor platform. The end walls of the platform building included attractive large windows with semi-circular heads. A small canopy extended over part of the platform, and the building was completed by a semi-hipped roof. This semi-hip roof lent to the building an appearance slightly reminiscent of some stations (such as those at Vowchurch and Dorstone) on the Golden Valley Railway (GVR) which had a sloping roof extension at each end of the main building. Similarly, the building at Almeley, and hence those on the New Radnor extension of the K&ER, were comparable with that at Clifford on the GVR.

Beyond the passenger station, and to the south of the bridge over the road, lay a goods siding, which was upgraded to a loop in 1928. Access was controlled from a small ground frame located in a timber building on the west side of the railway and released by the train staff. The loop was not used for crossing trains, since the whole of the line from Titley to Eardisley Junction constituted a single section worked on the one engine in steam principle. Road access to this goods siding was made via a short track leading from the main road.

Lyonshall station, looking south. The girder bridge and railings span the road (the present A480) from which access could be gained to the platform building. The hut beyond the bridge contains the ground frame controlling the points in the small goods yard.

John Alsop collection

A JOURNEY OVER THE LINES IN THE 1930s

The station buildings and platform at Almeley. *Tony Harden collection*

At 4 miles and 61 chains from Titley lay the station of Almeley. The main building on the platform here was simpler than that of its northern neighbour at Lyonshall: it consisted of a plain rectangular stone building with a pitched roof, and in these respects it was similar to those which were later provided on the New Radnor extension. To the south of this building, and also located on the platform, was a goods shed. As at Lyonshall, there was a small goods yard situated to the south of the passenger station and on the west side of the line. This was at one time a loop, with an additional siding, but from 1923 (just after the line was re-opened) there was a simpler arrangement with one long siding, the points for which were operated from a small ground frame housed in a hut and (as at Lyonshall) released by the train staff. Further south the line bridged the Coke's Yeld Dingle and then, shortly afterwards, the Holywell Dingle (both of which mainly lay on the north-west side of the line).

From the *massif* constituted by the hills lying to the south of the vale of the River Arrow there were commanding views of the meandering Wye and, more distantly, of Hay Bluff and of the Black Mountains. The Kington and Eardisley Railway now descended almost continuously and steeply all the way to Eardisley, running along banks and through cuttings freckled with wild flowers.

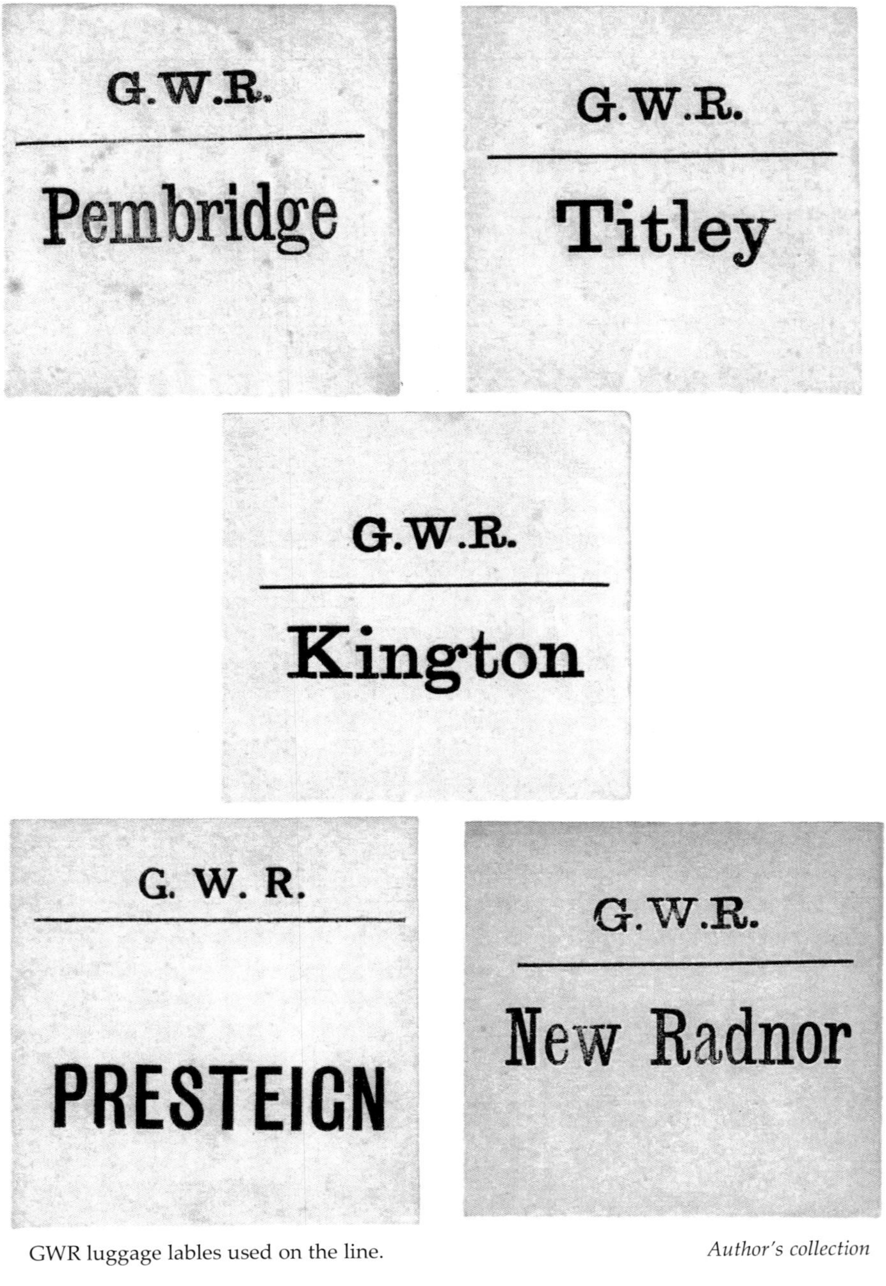

G.W.R.
Pembridge

G.W.R.
Titley

G.W.R.
Kington

G. W. R.
PRESTEIGN

G.W.R.
New Radnor

GWR luggage lables used on the line. *Author's collection*

Epilogue

The Kington lines formed a small but remarkable network set in one of the most remote parts of lowland Britain. Given the level of development in the district in the mid-nineteenth century, the establishment of a connection between Leominster and Kington was reasonable enough, but the other lines evinced a perhaps unwarranted optimism. In particular it seems clear that the Great Western Railway regarded the line between Titley and Eardisley as being superfluous, and it was only because of considerable local pressure by influential people that it was re-opened after its closure during the First World War. The advent of the Second World War provided a useful pretext for the final closure of this scenically beautiful but latterly little used line.

With the benefit of hindsight, it might have served the railway – and the district – better if the K&ER directors had sought to align themselves with the Midland Railway. Traffic from South Wales and Brecon might then have had a more direct route to Leominster and Shrewsbury, although the stiff gradients of the line to Titley would not have been favourable to the operation of heavy mineral trains, and, even had a direct connection between Lyonshall and Marston been made, it would still have been necessary for such trains to traverse the GWR line leading to Leominster.

There was a better case for the Presteigne line, serving the county town of Radnorshire. Here again, however, the sparseness of the passenger train service (at certain periods only two trains each way daily), taken with the necessity to change trains – once for Leominster, and twice for Ludlow or Hereford – was hardly likely to appeal to travellers who were not also railway enthusiasts.

Looking east from the overbridge at Eardisley Junction, 13th August, 1932. At this double junction the line veering to the left is the GWR line to Titley Junction and Kington. The line to Hereford goes straight ahead. *John Alsop collection*

The station at Kington was well placed in relation to the town, and a service of between five and seven trains daily to and from Leominster, with an average journey time of thirty five minutes, was in a stronger position to draw passengers; and, although not in the town centre, the railway station at Leominster was reasonably well sited. But, although slower for the end-to-end transit, a motor bus service from there to Kington was more suited to travel to and from, and between, the intermediate villages such as Kingsland, Eardisland, and Pembridge: it could take passengers to the heart of these places (and to stopping places in between), whereas the railway stations were comparatively isolated and to reach them often entailed a wearying walk. The background, was, moreover, one of a population in decline after the First World War. Agriculture was gradually becoming less labour intensive, and domestic service was becoming less usual. For at least some country dwellers, the towns offered employment which was both better paid and more secure.

Goods traffic underwent a comparable decline. Although technically immature and in some cases even primitive, road lorries and other vehicles had the great advantage of running door to door, gate to gate; and, little by little, the state of the roads was improved during the inter-war years. To its credit, the Great Western Railway made a game attempt by its 'country lorry' system to counter the trend to move from rail to road, and Kington became a hub for collection and delivery; and it opened two halts – at Forge Crossing and at Marston – in an effort to attract new passenger custom.

Nevertheless, the modal shift to road transport was in retrospect inevitable, and the petrol shortages of the Second World War and of its aftermath had the effect of only retarding rather than halting the inexorable growth of motor transport and of private car usage. For a while there remained certain traffics for which rail transport prevailed: in the case of the Kington lines there was the carriage of coal, and, above all, of stone and lime from the quarries and kilns west of Kington. Such traffic became the raison d'être of the Kington and Eardisley extension to Dolyhir, especially after it was realised that the longed-for westward extension beyond New Radnor to the Cambrian mountains and to the sea was unattainable. In the event, however, even this heavy mineral traffic was transferred to road vehicles, and it became sadly clear that the Kington lines were no longer needed for the carriage of freight.

Accordingly it is a matter for regret rather than for surprise that the Kington lines were, piece by piece, closed and dismantled. A few vestiges remain, mute witnesses to hope and endeavour.

Bibliography

Bartlett, S., *Hereford Locomotive Shed: Engines and Train Workings*, Pen and Sword Transport, 2017.

—— *Worcester Locomotive Shed: Engines and Train Workings*, Pen and Sword Transport, 2020.

Beck, K. M., *The West Midland Lines of the GWR*, Ian Allan, 1983.

Christiansen, R., *A Regional History of the Railways of Great Britain, Volume 13, Thames and Severn*, David and Charles, 1981.

—— *Forgotten Railways, Volume 11, Severn Valley and Welsh Border*, David and Charles, 1988.

Clark, R. H., *An Historical Survey of Selected Great Western Stations*, Volume Two, Oxford Publishing Company, 1979 (for Leominster station).

Clemens, M., *The Last Years of Steam around Central Wales*, Fonthill Media, 2015.

Clinker, C. R., 'The Worcester, Bromyard and Leominster Railway', in *The Railway Magazine*, 99 (1953), pp. 799 – 804.

—— 'The Railways of West Herefordshire', in *The Railway Magazine*, 103 (1957), pp. 599 – 605.

—— *The Hay Railway*, David and Charles, 1960.

Cook, R. *See under* Rattenbury, G.

Cooke, R. A., *Track Layout Diagrams of the Great Western Railway and B. R. Western Region, Section 63 Hereford*, published by the author, 1990.

de Courtais, Nicholas, *The New Radnor Branch*, Wild Swan Publications, 1992.

Dale, P., *Herefordshire and Worcestershire's Lost Railways*, Stenlake Publishing, 2004.

—— *Brecknock, Carmarthen and Radnor's Lost Railways*, Stenlake Publishing, 2005.

Fenn, R. W. D. See under Sinclair, J. B. and Fenn, R. W. D. (below).

Hadfield, C., *The Canals of South Wales and the Border*, 2nd Edition, David and Charles, 1967.

Harrison, I., *Great Western Railway Locomotive Allocations for 1921*, Wild Swan Publications, 1984.

Hewitt, J. D., 'The Kington Branch of the GWR', in *The Railway Magazine*, 85 (1939), pp.191 – 196.

Husband, J. F., 'Some Border Bye-ways of the Great Western Railway', in *The Railway Magazine*, 26 (1910), pp. 183 – 191.

Jenkins, S. C., 'The Bromyard Branch', in *Steam Days*, No. 113, (January, 1999), pp. 44 – 55.

—— 'The Leominster to New Radnor Branch', in *Steam Days*, No. 128 (April, 2000), pp. 199 – 211.

Lyons, E., and Mountford, E., *An Historical Survey of Great Western Engine Sheds, 1837 – 1947*, Oxford Publishing Company, 1979.

Lyons, E., *An Historical Survey of Great Western Engine Sheds, 1947*, Oxford Publishing Company, 1972.

Mair, J., *From Hereford to Three Cocks Junction*, The Oakwood Press, 2021.

Millward, R. and Robinson, A., *The Welsh Borders*, Eyre Methuen, 1978.

Mitchell, V. and Smith, K., *Branch Lines around Hay-on-Wye*, Middleton Press, 2007.

—— *Ludlow to Hereford, including the Kington Branch*, Middleton Press, 2007.

Morriss, R. K., *Rail Centres: Shrewsbury*, Ian Allan, 1986.

Mountford, E. *See under* Lyons, E.

Oldham, J. (editor), *The Diaries of Thomas Carleton Skarratt, Draper of Kington*, Herefordshire, privately published, 1987.

Oppitz, L., *Lost Lines of Herefordshire and Worcestershire*, Countryside Books, 2002.

Perkins, R. G., 'Presteigne [sic]: an ex-GWR station worth modelling', in *Model Railway Constructor*, May, 1969, pp. 152 – 153.

Rattenbury, G., and Cook, R., *The Hay and Kington Railways*, Railway and Canal Historical Society, 1996.

Robinson, A. See under Millward, R. and Robinson, A.

Sinclair, J. B. and Fenn, R. D. W., *The Facility of Locomotion: The Kington Railways*, Mid-Border Books, 1991.

Smith, W. H., *The Bromyard Branch from Worcester to Leominster*, Kidderminster Railway Museum, 1998.

—— *Herefordshire Railways*, Sutton Publishing Limited, 1998.

Thomas, D. St. J., *The Rural Transport Problem*, Routledge and Kegan Paul, 1963.

White, H. P., *Forgotten Railways*, David and Charles, 1986.

Wood, G., *Railways of Hereford*, Author, in conjunction with Kidderminster Railway Museum, 2003.

Index

Numbers in **BOLD** indicate an illustration.

Agricultural produce, 5, 58
Almeley, 25, 36, **36**, 37, 44, 89, 97, **97**; ground frame, 97; station buildings, 97
Ambulance trains, 39, 53
Auto-trains, 52

Banks, W L, 21
Bateman, Lady, 15
Bateman, William, 2nd Lord Bateman, 13, 16, 17
Board of Trade, 16, 25, 28, 30, 32
Bransford Road Junction, 33
Brassey and Field, 14, 15, 22, 49, 60
Brassey, Thomas, 11, 13; contract to run L&KR services, 19
Brecon, 4, 6, 9, 47, 48; Watton Wharf, 9, 89
Brecon & Abergavenny Canal, 4, 9
Brindley, James, 5
British Railways Western Region, 40, 63
Builth Wells, 27, 28
Burlingjobb, 4, 9, 26, 27, 28, 43, 89

Cambrian Railways, 24
Canals, 5, 6, 9
Cardigan Bay, 11
Central Wales Railway, 24, 94
Chambers, Charles, 25, 28, 59
Clarke, William, 95
Closure, 40; Dolyhir to New Radnor, 40; Titley to Eardisley, 39
Coal shortage, 40
Coal traffic, 5, 6, 9, 11, 14, 15, 58, 59
Craven Arms, 22, 23, 52

Davies, James, 14
Decline in passenger numbers, 36, 55
Devereux, Captain Walter, 20
Diesel railcar, 52, 56, 62
Dinmore tunnel, 11
Dolyhir, 21, 28, 41, 88, **90**, 91; freight traffic ends, 40; ground frame, 74, 91

Eardisley, 6, 9, 21, 22, 26, **26**, 44, 64, 89; Midland Railway treatment of GWR, 47, 48; potential for interchange station, 47; tram road junction, 6, 9
Eardisley Junction, 25, 75, **99**; signal box, 75
Evans, Thomas, 25

Field, William, 11, 13
First World War, 35, 49
Footbridges, 87
Forestry Commission, 39
Forge Crossing, 32, 38, 76, 83, 93, **93**
Frankland Lewis, Reverend Sir Gilbert, 59

Galton, Captain, 16
Golden Valley Railway, 96

Gradients, 43-44
Great Western Railway, 12, 19, 24, 25, 30, 31, 33, 34, 47, 61, 76, 99; Country Lorries, 38; motive power, 61-62
Green Price, Edith, 31

Hay Railway, 9, 20,; authorisation, 6; closure, 20
Hazledine and Sayce, 9
Hereford, 5, 6, 37, 63, 77; Barrs Court station, 11; Moorfields station, 16, 47; Barton station, 11, 47
Hereford and Gloucester Navigation Company, 6
Hereford, Hay and Brecon Railway, 9, 16, 20, 21, 26, 40, 46
Hergest, 39, 53
Hospitals, United States Army, 39, 53
Hutchinson, Colonel, 25, 30, 33

Iron products, 5, 58

Kingsland, **1**, 15, 18, **18**, 80, **80**; cattle pens, 81; crossing gatekeeper, 81; sawmill, 81; signal box, 68
Kington, 9, 15, 18, 41, **29**, 43, **48**, 53, 60, **85**, **86**, 99; accident, **42**; alteration to layout, 28-31; ; engine shed, 64, 87; Floodgates, 9, 88; population, 45; proposed branch canal, 5; proposed tram road to Leominster, 6; rebuilt station, 28, 74, 85, 86; signal box, 74; station buildings, 87; Sunset bridge, 64, 74, 88
Kington and Eardisley Railway, 21-26, 59; closed during wartime, 35, 39, 99; expansion plans, 22, 31, 82; extension to New Radnor, 27-28, 89; first sod, 22; gradients, 44; Lyonshall chord, 22, 31; motive power, 61; opening, 25, 43; passenger services, 46-49; reduced to carriage store, 75; Presteigne railway, 24, 25; reopened post-First World War, 36; reuse of Kington Railway alignment, 22; running powers, 25, 31
Kington Centenary Rail Tour, 41, **41**
Kington Junction, 13, 15, 67, 80
Kington Railway, 9, 14, 20, 26, 27, 33, 89; appeal for purchase, 14; authorisation, 9; clerk, 22; offer to buy shares, 21; petitions parliament, 14; rump Kington to Burlingjobb section, 22, 27; transhipment siding, 14
Knighton, 24, 35, 94

Ledbury, 5
Leominster, 5, 10, 48, 49, 52, 55, 77, 99; engine shed, 62-64, **62**, **76**, 78, **79**; first train to Kington, 17; services to Kington, 78; services via Bromyard, 49, 56, 78; signal box, **65**, 78; station enlarged, 63, 78
Leominster and Bromyard Railway, 34

103

Leominster and Kington Railway,   12-20; chairman,   13, 15; construction,   14-16; engineer,   13; first sod,   15; opening,   16-17, 43; passenger services,   17; Presteigne extension,   31; Royal Assent,   14; transhipment siding with Kington Railway,   14
Leominster Canal,   5, 12; part closed for railway,   11
Level crossings,   15, 67, 68, 70, 74, 76, 80, 81, 83, 88, 91; Kingsland gatekeeper,   81
Limestone and lime traffic,   4, 5, 9, 21, 26, 28, 58, 59, 89
Livestock,   58
Llangunllo,   24, 94
London and North Western Railway,   12
London, alternative routes,   56
Ludlow,   11, 52, 59, 77
Lugg Valley Railway,   24
Lyonshall,   22, 25, 31, 44, 89, 96, **96**; ground frame,   96

Marlbrook,   5
Marston,   18, 22, 43; chord to Lyonshall,   22, 31; new halt (siding),   38, 60, 82, 83, **83**
Meredith, John,   9
Midland Railway,   46, 47
Milford Haven,   20
Milk traffic,   46
Monmouthshire Canal,   6, 9
Motive Power,   60-62
Motor bus services,   37

Nationalisation,   39, 63
New Radnor,   **2**, 27, **27**, **30**, 32, 35, 48, 49, **52**, 55, 59, 64, 88, 91, **92**
New Radnor Extension,   26-28, 58, 59; opening,   30; passenger services,   31; working arrangements,   30; end of goods service,   60; end of passenger service,   40; ground frame,   93; signalling,   74; train turnaround,   56
Nieuport House,   36

Old Radnor,   59
Old Radnor Trading Company,   58, 59, 88, 91
Overend, Gurney and Company collapse,   24
Ox House private station,   18, 81

Passenger Rolling Stock,   49, 52
Passenger Services,   11, 17, 31, 38, 45-58; end of Leominster to Kington,   40; Pembridge 1936,   70, 82; scheduling at Eardisley,   48; suspended 1951,   40; wartime,   35, 39, 52-53
Pembridge,   15, 16, 18, 43, **71**, 81, **82**, 94; signal box,   69, 81; station master,   60, 70; unbuilt bridge,   15, 16, 81; West Ground Frame,   70
Perry and Company,   32
Presteigne,   22, 23, 24, 25, 31, **32**, 35, **37**, 41, 44, **60**, 64, 94, **94**; canopy removed,   95; cattle dock,   95; end of goods service,   60; end of

passenger service,   40; name,   4, 32, 41; signal box,   76
Presteigne Branch,   31-33, 93; bridge collapse,   33; false economies of route,   31; first sod,   31; gradients,   44; motive power,   61; opening,   33, 43,   ; working arrangements,   31, 33
Price, Thomas,   22
Proposed railways,   10, 23, **23**, 24, 27, 28, 92, 94

Rhayader,   27, 28
River; Arrow,   13, 27, 33, 80, 85; Lugg,   13, 43, 80; Severn,   5
Road competition,   38, 39
Robertson, Henry,   13

Savin, Thomas,   21, 22, 23; bankruptcy,   24
Second World War,   39, 52-53, 62
Shobdon airfield,   18, 81
Shobdon Court,   13, **13**, 18, 81
Shrewsbury,   11, 56, 64
Shrewsbury and Hereford Railway,   10-12, 63, 77, 95; authorisation,   10; passenger services start,   11
Signalling,   65-76; hours of operation,   76; methods,   65-66, 75
Smatcher, the,   91, **92**
Smeaton, John,   5
Speed restrictions,   76
Staffordshire and Worcestershire Canal,   5; River Lugg aqueduct,   5, 6
Stanner,   28, **58**, 88, **89**; downgraded to halt,   39; ground frame,   74
Station lighting,   83, 87, 88, 91, 92, 93, 95
Strinds Lime Works,   91
Suez Crisis,   39

Three Cocks Junction,   16, 47
Timber traffic,   37, 39
Titley Junction,,   15, 16, 18, 24, 25, 28, 31, 37, 43, 44, 45, 48, **73**, 83, 84, **84**, 93, 95; goods service withdrawn,   60; parallel lines,   32, 83; signal box,   72, 76, 84; signal box closed,   40, 72; simplified and track lifted,   40, 72, 93; water supply,   85
Tram road, proposed Leominster to Kington,   12
Tram roads,   6-10; gauge,   6

West Midland Railway,   12, 19, 49, 60
West Wales,   10, 20
Whitworth, Robert,   5
Woofferton,   5, 41, 56, 72, 78, 86
Wool and woollen goods,   5, 9, 58
Worcester,   10, 35, 63, 77; Shrub Hill,   33
Worcester, through trains from,   55
Worcester, Bromyard and Leominster Railway,   33-35; completed,   35; opened to Bromyard,   33
Wylie, David,   13, 95

Yolland, Colonel,   15

Scottish Beekeeping Handbook

A. Nicholas Cowan

Some justification is required for adding yet another book on beekeeping to the many on offer already. My first excuse is that I have been keeping bees in Scotland for thirty-five years, and Scottish conditions are a little different from those found in the south of England or in warmer climates. I have been mentoring people starting beekeeping for a number of years, and a book describing my methods could be useful to beginners and to others after I can no longer give instructions. An additional argument for another book is that I generally get a lot of honey from very few hives, and that was the reason given by one of my friends for referring me to the person who taught me most of the practical aspects of the craft many years ago. For several years I have also made nucleus stocks of bees available for people starting beekeeping, and for those who have unfortunately lost their bees and want to start again. This book gives instructions about how to set up small hives to provide bees for others and thus increase the numbers of honeybees and of beekeepers too.

My records show that I started beekeeping in 1978 and I have kept bees and records of their progress ever since. Soon after starting in the craft I took the courses recognised by the Scottish Beekeepers' Association and obtained the Beemasters' Certificate and the Apiarian Certificate. I would like to acknowledge the instruction given by the tutors, Bernard Mobus and Robert Couston and also members of the East of Scotland Beekeepers Association, particularly Jim Gray, and also George and James Braithwaite. Sadly, several of these expert beekeepers are no longer with us, but their valued instruction lives on, and I hope I have imparted some of their wealth of experience and knowledge of practical beekeeping in the pages which follow.

This booklet is mainly directed at beginners; it is concerned almost exclusively with the management of hives for honey production and the creation of new colonies of bees. Readers who want to know more about other aspects of beekeeping should make a search of their own into the vast number of books on bees and bee science in all aspects. I hope that some more experienced practitioners of the craft will also find in my booklet a few useful tips.

Although my beekeeping experience is mainly derived from Scottish conditions, the principles of beekeeping are appropriate for a wide variety of geographical and climatic conditions with slight modifications, taking account of when hives are likely to swarm, and when they will need extra feeding to aid survival in times of a dearth of nectar and pollen. I trust, therefore, that this booklet will be widely useful. Remember that it is one thing to 'have' bees, and something rather different to 'keep bees'. Too many novices lose their bees as a result of failing to manage the natural swarming instinct of bees, from failing to feed their bees when required, and from failure to treat diseases which are now common. If the instructions on the following pages lead to saving many bee colonies from extinction the author will be well pleased.

A. Nicholas Cowan. Midlothian, Scotland, 2014.

© A. Nicholas Cowan, 2014.
First published in the United Kingdom, 2014,
by Stenlake Publishing Ltd.
54–58 Mill Square,
Catrine, Ayrshire, KA5 6RD
Telephone: 01290 551122
www.stenlake.co.uk

ISBN 9781840336689